GOD BLESS THE CHILD

Also by James Colbert

GOD BLESS

THE

CHILD

James Colbert

ATHENEUM · NEW YORK · 1993

Maxwell Macmillan Canada
Toronto

Maxwell Macmillan International
New York   Oxford   Singapore   Sydney

Atheneum   Maxwell Macmillan Canada, Inc.
Macmillan Publishing Company   1200 Eglinton Avenue East
866 Third Avenue   Suite 200
New York, NY 10022   Don Mills, Ontario M3C 3N1

Macmillan Publishing Company is part of the Maxwell Communication
Group of Companies.

Library of Congress Cataloging-in-Publication Data
Colbert, James.
God bless the child/by James Colbert.
p. cm.
ISBN 0-689-12167-9
1. Gambling—Government policy—Mississippi. 2. Bingo—Government
policy—Mississippi. 3. Malone, Robert, 1954–. 4. Moore,
Michael C., 1952–. 5. Abused children—Services for—
Mississippi—Finance. 6. Hathorn, Sue, 1936–. 7. Children's
Advocacy Center (Jackson, Miss.) 8. Bingo—Law and legislation—
Mississippi. 9. Moore, Michael C., 1952—Trials, litigation, etc.
I. Title.
HV6721.M57C65 1993
364.1′72′09762—dc20   92–10076   CIP

Macmillan books are available at special discounts for bulk purchases for sales
promotions, premiums, fund-raising, or educational use. For details, contact:

Special Sales Director
Macmillan Publishing Company
866 Third Avenue
New York, NY 10022

10 9 8 7 6 5 4 3 2 1

Printed in the United States of America

This book is dedicated to Honey,
a very good and courageous friend
of a very good and courageous friend,
Alice Vachss

Them that's got shall get
    Them that's not shall lose
So the Bible said
    And it still is news;

Them that's strong gets more
    While the weak ones fade
Empty pockets don't ever make the grade;

Mama may have
    Papa may have
But God Bless the Child that's got his own,
    That's got his own.

GOD BLESS THE CHILD

ARTHUR HERZOG JR. AND BILLIE HOLIDAY
COPYRIGHT 1941 BY
EDWARD B. MARKS MUSIC COMPANY

For his help during both the writing of this book
and the preparation of the typescript
the author gratefully acknowledges David Hechler.

EXPLANATORY NOTE

The material in this book not derived from my own observations is taken from a variety of sources: official police and court records; interviews with persons directly or indirectly acquainted with specific individuals or events; newspaper and magazine accounts. Everything that follows is based on this carefully documented material. However, when the subject includes such emotionally loaded elements as the abuse of children, political expediency, and monetary gain it is to be expected that different points of view and shadings of the truth will be encountered. Whenever differences in accounts appeared, I considered and weighed information from all available sources before reaching my *own* conclusions. In some instances, I have reconstructed conversations and events; in places, I have transposed or otherwise clarified sentences in statements and remarks people have made. Throughout, however, I have made every effort not to alter meaning or significance or identity, with one notable exception: all names of abused children and of adult victims of child abuse have been changed and their identities altered to protect the privacy of those very many whom so few have tried so hard to protect.

GOD BLESS THE CHILD

PREFACE

The tables have been placed end to end in rows that run from front to back in the huge hall. Overhead, there are banks of bright fluorescent lights. The floors are waxed and polished to a bright, mirrorlike shine. Earlier, there had been a long line of people waiting to enter the hall. The line extended from the rear counter across the rear wall and out into the parking lot in a quiet, orderly, mostly single-file procession; but now those people—about sixteen hundred of them—are seated at all those tables. It takes ten minutes just to walk around them, to walk the perimeter of the hall. Now, between games, many have their arms straight up, fingers outstretched, one- or five- or ten-dollar bills held high. There is so much money waving in the air that from down low, from table height, the motion brings to mind a mature crop of wheat waving in the wind. Runners come and collect the bills, make change, sell cards. There is a sense of mounting excitement and anticipation. There is little noise.

Suspended from the ceiling there are video monitors and less easily observed—video cameras. On the front wall, above and behind the stage, there is a scoreboardlike sign that displays numbers. On that same wall, to the left of the sign, there is a door that leads to the manager's office. The door opens and closes often, on average perhaps once every sixty seconds.

In that office there is one long, rectangular table, just like the tables out front, and at a right angle to the table there is a gray metal desk. Next to the desk, a two-way mirror gives a view out into the hall. On the corner of the desk there is a silver pistol. In the corner, within easy reach, there is a short-barreled pump-action shotgun. The runners come in one at a time, dump the cash from the pockets of their aprons, take more cards. The two people sitting behind the table sort the bills by denomination, count them, wrap them in rubber bands, pass them to the man behind the desk. The keys of an adding machine click softly, worked rapidly. For hours, the counting is continuous, the sound of crinkling money uninterrupted. The desk is literally covered with banded sheaves of bills. In the corner by the shotgun, a third pasteboard box fills with money, then a fourth.

The man behind the desk is named Robert Malone. He is thirty-six years old. His nose is short, the nostrils flared, hawklike in a round, owl face. He is wearing a gold-coin ring, a gold ID bracelet, and a shirt unbuttoned to reveal a gold chain. His hair is neatly styled, parted on the left. When from behind his heavily tinted gold-frame glasses he glances up, it is easy to have the sense that he is sighting down the barrel of the shotgun. His eyes are very blue and very hard, quick to focus in a flat, demanding stare. He takes a pull on his cigarette, looks to his left, scans the video monitors that show the action in the hall.

"Fucking bingo," he says, as if he can't quite believe it himself; then he carelessly tosses a thick wad of bills at one of the boxes in the corner. "*Bingo.*"

The tension in the room is palpable, almost tangible, growing as more boxes are filled with money. This one night's gross will exceed one hundred fifty thousand dollars, all of it cash, most of it in small, used bills.

From the hall there is a roar. A woman has just won the cover-all.

Robert Malone exhales smoke through his nose.
"Still think bingo is so quaint and cute?"
Not everyone does.

In the parking lot behind the government-modern, three-story office building many of the cars are new. Parked among the Buicks and the Fords there are BMWs and customized Jeeps and slick Japanese sports cars. Going from that parking lot up the ramp that leads inside, almost without exception the men wear single-breasted suits, blue or white solid-color shirts with button-down collars, conservative ties, lace-up shoes or loafers. The hems of women's dresses fall to mid-calf. The elevator moves slowly, stopping at every floor.

Given the enormous power of the official who occupies the office on the top floor, the trappings both are and are not what you might expect. On the floor there is an industrial-grade tan carpet. The walls are dark paneling. Fluorescent lights are inset into the low ceiling, the light diffused by plastic panels. In the reception area, there are two desks and, for visitors, two boxy, black leather chairs. Hung on the walls there are paintings of a fox, a country road, a swamp scene; near the door to the inner office there is the Great Seal of the state. The ceiling of the inner office is considerably higher than the ceiling of the outer office. The scale is grander. Large plate-glass windows offer an expansive view of the state capitol just across the street. The capitol building is huge and impressive, the grounds beautifully kept, the view of it as eye-filling, as mesmerizing and as seductive as ambition.

Mike Moore is thirty-eight years old. He is the youngest Attorney General ever to occupy that office. He is the chief legal officer (or as he interprets it, the chief *law enforcement* officer) for the state. His staff reflects what is very nearly a theme of the office: it is hard to spot a face over forty.

Youth and power.

From here Mike Moore takes the elevator to the first floor

and enters the courtroom of the Supreme Court of the state of Mississippi. He is wearing a blue shirt, darker blue tie, gray suit. His face is long, almost gaunt, framed by wavy hair brushed straight back from his forehead, carefully styled. He has a thin, chiseled face, boyish good looks. There is a crowd gathered near the door to the courtroom. Inside, every seat is taken. Mike Moore shakes hands all around on his side of the court; he waves at the opposing table. When arguments are made, he will tuck his upper lip between his teeth and chew it, change from one earnest look to another, head cocked, eyes down, then up. Directly behind him sits his newly hired media consultant, Stephanie Bell, formerly the anchor of the local news, eye-catchingly blond, vivacious, and young.

The arguments to be made before the Supreme Court this day both are and are not about bingo. What is really at stake is the state-run lottery proposed by the governor. Mike Moore and his assistants will argue that bingo is itself a lottery and therefore not permitted by the state constitution. Unless the constitution is changed, he will maintain, neither bingo nor a lottery is legal. To keep bingo, therefore, the lottery must be approved. It is a position that has incurred the wrath of every bingo-playing charity in the state—and there are many, those same groups politicians most times are so careful to cultivate, the Shriners, the United Catholic Charities, the Knights of Columbus, the American Legion, AmVets, the International Ballet Competition, Disabled American Veterans, the Special Olympics. The commander of the state Veterans of Foreign Wars is quoted as saying, "Mike Moore has just committed political suicide." The local paper reports that "some legislators were suspicious of the timing of Moore's move." It is, at the very least, a rather curious tactic politically. Mike Moore says it is all "purely coincidental."

At one table, Robert Malone's attorney sits by himself preparing to argue against the Attorney General and what appears to be the entire assembled staff of the Attorney General's Office. The courtroom is packed, but there is complete, ear-ringing silence. Not a single throat is cleared. There is not a single hushed aside. What is at stake for Robert Malone is the next forty-five years of his life, the maximum penalty for the racketeering and contempt with which he has been charged. What is at stake for the state of Mississippi, by many measures the poorest state in the country, is the creation of what is potentially a *sixty- to one-hundred-million-dollar-per-year cash industry*.

Youth and power. And money.

Robert Malone sits up straight in his seat. His cheeks are flushed crimson. His hands are clasped together tightly in his lap. It is obvious he would prefer to be almost anywhere else. Just for a moment he glances at the gray-haired woman one seat away from him. In his glance there is anger, expectation, uncertainty, hope. The woman smiles back at him in an oblivious, benign fashion, as if she cannot quite comprehend what is going on but is certainly hoping for the best, as if she is unaware that *she* has set the stage for this confrontation, the decision of which will very directly affect the lives of literally tens of thousands of people.

The woman's name is Sue Hathorn. She is fifty-three years old but seems to try to appear older. She is wearing a bright red blazer over a bright red skirt. Her blue-gray hair is coiffed in a neat grandmotherly fashion. It is easy to picture her in her house, placing the linens just so, carefully dusting the furniture, displaying the doilies and quilts she got from her mother. She seems your basic, gray-haired, churchgoing, elemental southern lady, but Sue Hathorn has a core inside her hard as rolled steel. What Sue Hathorn has decided is that she is going to help the abused children of Mississippi. To get the money to do that, she joined forces with Robert Malone and now stands with him in opposition to the state Attorney General. What those around her—including Robert Malone—have underestimated is the strength of her resolve, her willingness to forge ahead, to have her way, whatever the cost.

The bailiff calls, "All rise," as the nine justices—eight men and one woman—enter.

Before the Supreme Court renders its decision on an expedited schedule, at least two children in Mississippi will be brutally murdered. Over two hundred others will be reported abused, physically or sexually, though the actual rate of incidence is certainly far higher than the number reported.

Sue Hathorn, that oblivious, benign expression fixed on her face, thinks about one child, then another, knowing each one of them is directly subject to the huge, complex forces at work in that courtroom that day.

"We are surrounded," she says to herself, her litany. "We can attack in any direction."

Whatever the cost.

Robert Malone and Mike Moore, they just *think* they know about gambling. They are both about to learn.

What nine-year-old Tricia Alexander has learned is something else entirely.

She has learned about terror.

The large, square room in the renovated old house has high ceilings, but the furniture is small and low, scaled for children. Through the big double-hung windows sunlight streams in. On the floor there is a thick, comfortable carpet, well padded, good for sitting. On shelves, on the floor, in corners, there are dolls and toys and games of every imaginable description. The room is cheerful, a bright, happy room for children, comfortably cluttered but neat, the colors and the textures soft, a place designed so they will feel relaxed and safe. In all four corners, up high, there are video cameras placed to cover every square inch of the room. On the other side of the wall, in a room that was once a pantry, there is an impressive array of sophisticated electronic equipment, monitors, amplifiers, control panels, wireless microphones, and miniature two-way radios. When the girl enters, picks out a stuffed toy and begins to play with it, talking to it, in the viewing room there is an uncomfortable sense of spying, of intruding on private moments.

A woman enters. Careful to drop down when she approaches the little girl, she sits on her heels before she sits on the carpet, her legs folded beneath her. She begins to repeat for the little girl what it is apparent they have gone over before, that this is the interview, that they are being videotaped. The woman's face is serene and reassuring, but very focused. The little girl nods her understanding but does not look away from the toy. She is nine years old. Her baby-fine blond hair has a reddish tint to it. Her complexion is very white, very fair, with a smattering of freckles across her nose. A few minutes later, at the woman's urging, the little girl sits at the desk and draws a picture, using crayons to color a plain white sheet. The picture is of a landscape, an open field, the sun, the sky; but the little girl uses all reds and grays and blacks to draw it, slashing at the paper, a heavy pressure on the crayons. The drawing is disturbing in its intensity, a vision of a post-apocalyptic, nightmare world, the huge anger evident even to the untrained eye.

The woman's voice is soothing and firm, assured yet not challenging. She looks at the drawing, asks if she can have it, dates and initials it; then she points to several humorous-looking dolls nearby, dolls made to resemble men and women and children.

"Show me what happened," the woman says.

"Happened when?" the little girl replies.

"That time in the park," the woman says softly. "We can start there."

A dark look passes over the little girl's face. After a moment, she gets up, picks out two of the dolls, returns to the center of the room, begins to undress the dolls, a man and a little girl.

"This is my daddy," she says, removing the clothes from the first doll in a matter-of-fact way.

"My new daddy."

The doll is anatomically correct; it has both hair and genitals. She tosses it aside and picks up the other.

In the viewing room, the light from the video monitor plays across Sue Hathorn's face. Her expression is not so oblivious now, not so benign.

7

"This is me," the little girl says, furiously ripping the clothes off the little-girl doll. The same intensity is evident in her face that was in her drawing, a rage. She begins to mash the naked dolls together, face to face.

Political maneuverings, struggles for money, plays for power, they are all there in that room, colliding as violently as those naked, overstuffed dolls. Before it is over, in this case, there will be a winner and a loser—and a lot more business as usual.

PROLOGUE

Jackson is both the capital of and the largest city in the state of Mississippi, the Magnolia State. At first glance, it appears to be just one of those sleepy little southern towns grown up along the two interstate highways that intersect there, I-55 and I-20, to a population of over 200,000. Coming in along I-55 you see Capitol Towers with its reflective bronze glass and IOF Foresters sign on top, the old state capitol, the brick Trustmark Building, the Deposit Guaranty Bank Building, at twenty-two stories the tallest building in the state, the high-rise Holiday Inn, and a little ways away, obscured behind the Ramada Inn's Coliseum, the new state capitol and, next to the Carroll Gartin Justice Building, the Sillers Building. Downtown, these newer buildings overshadow the old home of Standard Life, the old and abandoned King Edward Hotel next to the Noble Hotel ("reasonable rates"), the beautiful Greek Revival governor's mansion. As in so many other small American cities, on workdays downtown is bustling, alive with activity; but at night and on weekends it is very nearly abandoned, the coat-and-tie crowd having fled to the various suburbs.

On East Capitol Street, down from the stately old capitol,

now a museum, near where the monolithic Dr. A. H. McCoy Federal Building sits across from the vaguely modern U.S. Bankruptcy Court, there is an all-night café that is pure 1950s, Bauhaus with a deco influence, all plastic and chrome. In a high-backed booth and on two of the round chrome stools at the room-length counter, this night there sit three people: a policeman, a visitor, obviously staying at one of the hotels nearby, obviously wondering where the city went when it got dark, and a black street person, spending the coins he has collected during the day on the hamburger-steak dinner special. Both the street person and the policeman—though each from his own very different perspective—know where the city is after dark. It is in the low-income area literally across the tracks, three blocks away. It is in the roadhouses out on the highway, in the four hundred or so mostly Baptist churches in the area, in the middle-class suburbs set among huge oaks and, of course, magnolias. Life in Jackson is most often described as "nice" or "pleasant," and it is both like and unlike other southern cities its size, though why this city is there at all is a little bit more difficult to determine.

"Mississippi begins with wonder," reads the opening line of the official state brochure. "For more than the land it occupies, more than the facts of history, Mississippi begins with a feeling that there is more about this place than the senses can convey"—and that is true for the city of Jackson as well, though not, most likely, as the Secretary of State meant it when he wrote those words.

Jackson is one of the first planned cities in the United States, a fact evidenced by the tight, regular Jeffersonian grid that makes up downtown. But other than a low bluff that rises about twenty feet above the floodplain of the Pearl River, there really is no good reason for the city to be there, no natural port or geographic center, certainly no ocean, nothing that "the senses can convey." The city was, in fact, founded to end a political dispute begun in 1798 that was not finally resolved until 1821, a squabble between Federalists and planter Republicans about where to locate the territorial capital. The first inhabitants of Jackson were government officials. The town was named after a statesman, even before it was a town. Its tenuous, unlikely existence was sustained only by the annual meetings of the state legislature. So even before its inception, even more than on Le Fleur's Bluff (which even Mr. Le Fleur abandoned for a better location), Jackson was founded on partisan politics, disputes between the haves and the have-nots—or, more accurately, between the haves and the disenfranchised, a distinction even then made not simply by race.

There is a photograph, taken in 1905, that shows the new state capitol just after it was completed. Modeled after the national capitol, complete with gold-leafed eagle, ornate dome, and Italian marble, there it sits in all its Beaux Arts Classical majesty among dirt roads and a few widely scattered, ramshackle wood-frame buildings. In the foreground, a black man leads a mule-drawn cart. The huge, pristine building looks so out of place it appears to have survived some sort of devastation, more like one of those chance survivors of Dresden or Tokyo than a new construction. Certainly there must have been other buildings around it at one time—but there never were. The devastation occurred forty years before, during the Civil War, when Jackson was burned three times by Union troops under the command of William Tecumseh Sherman. General Sherman's troops did such a thorough job only the brick chimneys of the town remained standing, and for a time Jackson was known as Chimneyville. In this photograph that rubble has been cleared away, but the obvious devastation remains. This new capitol was built at a cost of one million dollars at a time when a million dollars really was a huge amount of money, at a time when the state and even the city itself were unreconstructed. As a symbol of a social dynamic, as representative of where priorities are placed, the new capitol has proved amazingly durable, as up to date today as the day it was completed.

Prologue

"This is what the people want," claimed the governor seeking to build the new capitol, apparently not looking out the window of the old capitol.

In any event, it is certainly what they got.

The area profile compiled by the Mississippi Department of Economic and Community Development states that "Mississippi's per capita state and local taxes are the lowest in the nation," which seems credible given the unmentioned fact that, according to the U.S. Bureau of Economic Analysis, per capita income is also the lowest in the United States. One out of five people in the state of Mississippi lives below poverty level; one out of five births is to a teen mother. In Jackson, there are only 213 dentists to serve a population of over 200,000. Yet there are, as well, ten eighteen-hole golf courses. There is a symphony orchestra, a professional ballet company, two opera companies, theater, and the International Ballet Competition. There are twenty-three banks. Government, somehow not surprisingly, is the city's largest employer, continuing a long tradition in this city founded on politics—on disputes between the haves and the disenfranchised.

Not too far from the now not-so-new state capitol, just down the block from the Carroll Gartin Justice Building, in the parking lot of the Mississippi State Fair then underway, an event so small occurred that it was likely unnoticed even by the fairgoers passing just a few feet away. A young man and a middle-aged woman got out of a car, and as they went to secure the woman's purse in the trunk, they spotted two aluminum cans on the ground. The woman was Sue Hathorn, the director of the Mississippi Committee for the Prevention of Child Abuse. The young man was Jeff Johns, her part-time assistant, then twenty-one years old. At that time, October 1989, both were constantly on the lookout for aluminum cans, since the fee the recycling company paid for them was a much needed part of the operating budget of the MCPCA, a fledgling, certainly

12

nonprofit organization. What the MCPCA offered was mainly referrals and counseling. Any caregiver, any individual family, anyone who felt he had a problem or was not getting justice was encouraged to call or to come by the modest office in the Barefield Complex, the one limitation being that the services MCPCA provided were restricted to helping a child. Referrals were made by state agencies, by schoolteachers and social workers, by those previously helped. The money that made this service possible was provided by subscriptions to the organization's newsletter, *Mississippi Voices*, by donations, by grants, and by recycling aluminum cans—a fact attested to by the bags of cans stashed in the office's closets and in Sue Hathorn's garage.

Sue Hathorn had recently returned from a visit to Huntsville, Alabama, a trip that had changed her life. In Huntsville, a progressive district attorney had created a Children's Advocacy Center, a center where professionals from all disciplines involved with child sexual abuse worked together to help rather than to revictimize children by bouncing them from one agency to another. Policemen, social workers, prosecuting attorneys, medical workers, teachers, all had a warm, nonthreatening environment in which to determine the best course of action for the child—and to interact among themselves and stave off the burnout so common in the field. Sue Hathorn wanted such a center for Jackson, but she knew that in the climate that had prevailed in her city for over a century and a half, she had better figure out a way to pay for it herself. Heck, the children didn't have a voice. Who could hear them? They couldn't even vote.

She picked up the two aluminum cans and put them in the trunk of her car.

Before she shut the trunk lid, Jeff Johns moved them nearer to her purse.

Not understanding why Jeff had put the smelly, still wet cans right beside her purse, she looked at him questioningly.

"I don't want you to forget them," Jeff explained. Though dressed in his customary dark suit and tie and very self-possessed

13

for his age, at that moment he looked his tender years. "Why, Sue," he went on, "what would happen if my momma found beer cans in the trunk of my car?"

Sue Hathorn began to laugh, thinking of all that Jeff's question conveyed, a light chuckle that contained genuine good humor and resignation, a momentary release from her certain knowledge of the life-or-death struggles always near at hand.

"God help me," she said, at that moment believing that He would, if only she could find a way to help herself, though who under the kingdom of heaven would ever have guessed that help would come in the form of high-stakes bingo and Robert Malone?

CHAPTER

1

It was hot that day. It was the middle of summer in Mississippi, hot and muggy, the air itself a thick, heavy presence. Nearby there was a lake, and it was fun to wade out into it, to feel the cool water come up past her knees, to splash it onto her arms, to feel the squishy mud between her toes. Tricia felt safe at the water's edge because there were people there. Others. Twice, a ski boat had gone past, engine whining, hull thumping, planing and bouncing, behind it a smell of spray and exhaust intermixed and a chorus of exhilarated shouts.

Her mother was stretched out on a full-length lawn chair, the folding kind made from aluminum and brightly colored straps. She was lazing in the sun, and Tricia knew that when her mother got up, there would be impressions from the straps on her skin, funny horizontal bands across her back and the backs of her legs. When her mother called out to her and asked her to go to the cooler to get her a drink, Tricia did not know how to tell her the fear that brought, the terror that lurked in the shadows from the tall pine trees that came practically down to the edge of the water. If she was quick, she thought, she could make it. If she ran.

The path that led into the trees was bare gray earth covered in places by rust-red pine needles. It was quiet among the trees, away from the water, quiet and gray and spooky.

She hurried.

Before her mother and she had gone on down to the water, the three of them had eaten lunch at one of the tables the park provided. They had picnicked on fried chicken and potato salad and coleslaw, her mother, her stepfather, and she. This was where they had left the cooler, near the table.

Tricia watched her step, looking out for broken glass or pop-tops or the occasional root that snaked across her path. As she neared the table, she looked around, eyes wide, alert for danger; but she saw nothing and advanced cautiously. Quietly, she flipped open the red cooler's white top. Her hand was deep down in the icy-cold water when she felt a huge arm across her middle, felt herself being lifted up. The can slipped from her grasp.

"Gotcha," her stepfather said, smirking, his huge face near to hers.

The terror was there with the anger.

Powerlessness.

Next to her he was a giant. He talked the whole time, his voice mean, edged with threat.

"You came to see me, didn't you?" he asked. "You like this, don't you?"

The limbs of the trees were high overhead, bright sunlight sparkling behind them. His fingers were fat and strong, with coarse hair on them and grease from the chicken, groping, pulling her elasticized swimsuit away from her flesh, away from her gawky, unformed body. Beneath her back she felt the hard, rough concrete of the table, cold as a slab, slimy with green mildew. The air intruded. Her legs were skinny as sticks, pulled apart.

"Doesn't that feel good?" her stepfather asked. His breath smelled of beer.

She could not possibly reply. It hurt. Her rage and her humiliation were too big for words. She struggled; then she remembered what her mother had told her. "You be good to this man, Tricia. He's good to us. He works hard to give us what we need. The least you can do is to be nice to him. He's our last chance."

Tricia heard the ski boat. She heard her mother's voice, calling, far away. She couldn't let her mother know. She couldn't.

Among other things, what was to be determined was whether her mother already did.

2

It was the sixth of January 1990, the start of a new year, and while in years past Sue Hathorn had done some onerous things for money—begging donations, completing the ridiculous amount of paperwork required to receive grants, fishing for aluminum cans—*this*, she was convinced, was without doubt the strangest thing she had ever done. Fortunately, she had been here before, to this Bingo Depot, and knew at least partly what to expect. Even though it was after ten o'clock at night, the shopping center's vast parking lot was completely filled. There wasn't a parking place within three hundred yards of the door.

Back in November, Sue had first learned from a friend about the man named Robert Malone. She had learned that, by state law, in order to operate legally the proceeds from a bingo game had to go to a charity, and because of that law Malone was always on the lookout for places to spend his bingo money. Well, she could help him out there. What she needed at the moment was six thousand dollars to be eligible for county matching funds to start up a Court-Appointed Special Advocate (CASA) program, which would train volunteers to help children get through their days in court. And she had tried to ask him—more than once, in fact—but the man had been insistent: come see my bingo game, *then* we'll talk.

So she had.

What she had expected was a bunch of little old ladies in a room somewhere, probably in a church or a school auditorium, moving kernels of corn around on stiff, reusable cardboard cards. What she had found instead was an enormous, brightly lit hall filled to capacity, people of all ages and descriptions—black, white, young, old, professional, blue-collar, men and women—playing bingo with a mind-boggling intensity. The games, she had been told, began at five in the afternoon for the early birds and went on to five in the morning. During that time, the players used up over five thousand pounds of ice in their soft drinks. They went through a hundred twenty-five loaves of bread for their sandwiches. They put sixty gallons of nacho cheese on their chips. They drank over four hundred gallons of coffee. And they marked up over two hundred thousand sheets of the disposable bingo paper, enough to fill to overflowing the truck-sized blue Dumpster out back. And if that wasn't crazy enough, this Robert Malone had sat her down next to a woman he had claimed was his mother.

Well, she had tried.

She had tried because she wanted that money, but by midnight she was so bored that despite all the activity—the numbers being called, the dozens of runners dashing down the aisles, the cheers and elation when somebody won—she was falling asleep at the table. She just couldn't understand it. Why would anyone spend good money to mark up a sheet of what looked like newsprint? But she *had* done the one thing she had set out to do. She had met Robert Malone, if only for about two seconds, and that was all the opening she needed. Come Monday, she knew, she would be on the phone to him, and Tuesday, too, and Wednesday and Thursday and Friday, whatever it took, though she hadn't quite counted on that trip to his office.

Handy Avenue. She'd been down it before but hadn't

stopped there. Why would she? There wasn't anything there but liquor stores of the sort people hung around to do their drinking, vacant lots where the weeds had grown up waist high, motels available by the hour or the week, a few restaurants so run-down it looked like the grease had soaked right through the walls. But that's where her six thousand dollars was, and that's where she went.

Where she turned there was some sort of business that needed a high razor-wire-topped chain-link fence around it, a place where it looked like they let a bad dog loose at night. Where she turned again there were two rows of prefabricated metal buildings built facing in, making their own alley. She had taken Jeff Johns with her, and his only comment had been "Oh my God." But they hadn't even gotten in yet and seen what was inside. With its metal walls and bare concrete floor, the place was damp and cold, like a warehouse, and it just *looked* suspicious. There were boxes of bingo paper stacked floor to ceiling. There were VCRs and video poker machines haphazardly placed. There was an industrial-strength paper cutter so surgical in its appearance it looked like it belonged in a hospital. There were stacks of magazines about gambling and catalogues of gambling supplies. In the small office itself there was a computer hooked up to a high-speed printer that was printing nonstop, spitting and stuttering. And then there by himself was Robert Malone wearing all that gold and polyester pants and tinted glasses and behind them his eyes hard as marbles.

"How much do you want?" he had asked her, coming right to the point.

"Six thousand dollars," she had replied, resolute.

"Okay," he had said, just like that. "Come by the Depot the first Saturday of next month."

"I'll be there," Sue had said, momentarily elated, then wondering just what it was she had gotten herself into.

Back in the car, Jeff had begun, "Now, Sue—"

"We got our money," she had cut him off; then the next month she went to Bingo Depot, by God, to collect it.

And it went pretty well, she thought. At the intermission Robert Malone called her up on the stage and presented her with the check, though it seemed they were the only two people in the room interested in any way at all. Monday morning she was at the bank first thing, making the deposit, making sure the check was, in fact, good, and for the next few days she hadn't thought much about it, except to wonder when she could hit the bingo man up for more money. Then on Thursday morning she opened up the *Clarion-Ledger* and got the shock of her life.

She thought she was having a stroke.

Right there on the front page of the newspaper was a big headline and a picture: Bingo Depot had been raided. In the picture two men in dark jackets were walking the aisles. The hall very obviously had been hastily abandoned. On the tables there were partially marked bingo cards and half-filled beverage containers. On the backs of the men's jackets big letters read: NARCOTICS POLICE. In front of them was the stage where she had accepted the check only five days before.

"God help me," she said, but this time she could not force a chuckle behind it.

"Jackson police raided a bingo parlor Wednesday night," the article began. "Attorney General Mike Moore claimed the Bingo Depot is netting a million dollars a year," the article went on. "'I don't know of a charity that's received that much money,' the Attorney General said."

Sue Hathorn sat up straight in her chair.

"A million dollars a year," she read again. Why, she had only gotten six thousand.

3

On the thirteenth floor of the Deposit Guaranty Bank Building, one of the newer buildings that make up downtown Jackson, on the afternoon of January 11, 1990, Mike Farrell stood in a corner conference room, momentarily looking out at the view of the city the big windows provided—a view that looked away from the other new buildings and away from the state capitol. Taking his tie between his thumb and first finger, he smoothed the material, a habitual adjustment he was not really aware of. He also smoothed down the hair on the back of his head. He was trying to order his thoughts because the events that had occurred in the previous twenty hours were the most bizarre in his fifteen-year legal career, though he had to admit he had little experience with criminal law, only enough, he would say, to be dangerous. And at that point he had to assume that the proceedings were criminal, though he didn't know that for a fact. No one, it seemed, knew much of anything—at least, they weren't telling *him*. He started to get himself a cup of coffee from the carafe kept on the side table but thought better of it. He started to go back to his office but thought better of that, too.

Mike Farrell is a native Mississippian. He went to Laurel High School and Mississippi State before going on to Georgetown Law School. He is married, the father of four, the owner of a toy fox terrier dog and a house in the Bellhaven section of Jackson. In that corner conference room he appears completely at ease among the subdued though expensive fabrics, the quiet prints, the restrained atmosphere you would expect of a successful, sixteen-lawyer law firm that handles mostly business and commercial litigation. Mike Farrell is so soft-spoken that at times he seems timid, almost shy. He is well built, compact, though he will tell you that he still needs to lose a couple more pounds. He is, arguably, the most unlikely lawyer in the state of Mississippi to represent Robert Malone, a fact not lost on him at all. But in his quiet manner he was angry, too, angry about the way both he and his client had been treated, angry about the cavalier, abusive treatment given them, and he had to admit he wanted the case.

What had happened was this: At eight-thirty the previous evening he had still been at work when Robert Malone called him and told him that some sort of raid was going on at Bingo Depot. Mike Farrell didn't have a car there at his office—his wife had dropped him off that morning—and Robert had had to send someone to get him. At Bingo Depot, because there were camera crews at the front door, he had gone in through the back and discovered a mildly chaotic scene that included highway patrolmen, Jackson policemen, a few leftover bingo patrons, representatives from the Attorney General's Office, an assistant city district attorney, and, of course, Robert Malone. A man with a video camera was walking the aisles, taping everything. Other people were making an inventory of the Depot's contents. What had impressed Mike Farrell first was that an assistant district attorney was there at the scene, making himself a part of the case; and right after that there were the papers with which Robert had been served, a criminal search warrant and a civil lawsuit, which didn't make any sense at all— even a rookie paralegal knew that there was supposed to be a strict separation between criminal and civil proceedings. After a while, at the desk at the front of the hall, he had found Don Bartlett, the chief of detectives of Jackson PD, who had told him that he was in charge.

"So," Mike Farrell had asked, "what are your intentions?"

"We're going to clean it out," Don Bartlett had replied. "Wall to wall."

"Tonight?" Mike Farrell had asked, joking, because it was, after all, a mighty big hall.

"We're going to start tonight," the chief of detectives replied dourly. "If we can move it or unbolt it, we're taking it."

And they had.

Mike Farrell had watched for a while, growing more and more perplexed as they moved the tables, the chairs, even the water fountain. They unbolted the air cleaners from the ceiling. Finally, he had gone up to Ralph Holliman, one of the Attorney General's representatives at the scene.

"This is crazy," he had protested.

In reply, Ralph Holliman had given him an enigmatic smile, but other than that smile, Mike Farrell's protest was met with no other response whatsoever.

Because the chief of detectives of Jackson PD, Don Bartlett, had told him that he was in charge, the next day Mike Farrell spoke to Tim Hancock, the City Attorney for the city of Jackson. Tim Hancock told him he had spoken with both Don Bartlett and the mayor of Jackson and both had informed him that the entire operation against Robert Malone and Bingo Depot was under the control of the Attorney General's Office. They were just taking orders from the Attorney General. But before Mike Farrell could even puzzle that out, wondering why

Ralph Holliman hadn't informed him of that, the receptionist buzzed him to announce two surprise visitors, Jim Warren and Tim Waycaster from the Attorney General's Office.

Good, Mike Farrell thought.

"Send them in," he said to the receptionist.

In the corner conference room the men shook hands all around, introducing themselves, very friendly.

"We're hoping," Jim Warren began, "maybe we can work this out."

Mike Farrell thought that over for a moment, deciding which step to take first.

"We've talked to the police department about not moving the equipment out of the Depot," he said, starting with the point that concerned his client the most. "And frankly, I've got some real problems with the search warrant."

Jim Warren gave him an enigmatic smile. "I'm sorry," he replied. "Our office has nothing to do with that end of it."

"But I just spoke with the city attorney," Mike Farrell said. "He told me that the whole operation was under your control."

Jim Warren threw up his hands, still smiling, the only answer he would give.

Which was why late on that Thursday afternoon Mike Farrell was standing at that corner window smoothing his tie and his hair, trying to make sense of events that, so far, made no sense at all. He remembered what Robert Malone had asked of no one in particular as he watched his business being dismantled. "Will someone kindly tell me just what the fuck is going on here?" And while that language was not the sort Mike Farrell himself would have chosen, the question did pretty much strike to the heart of the matter.

With Jim Warren and Tim Waycaster's visit, Mike Farrell had the sense that the two were sizing up the opposition, following up on the opening salvo in what he considered a very questionable operation.

Among those who think such good ole boy courtesy calls

are effective, a way of soft-pedaling very hard business, it will not be surprising that Jim Warren and Tim Waycaster thereafter neglected a fairly fundamental rule of engagement: after the opening shot is fired, it is best to watch very closely to see how that shot is received, whether the target turns tail and runs or hunkers down and comes at you full speed.

4

*T*he classroom was one large square room with a high ceiling, a friendly, comfortable place. There were big windows on both sides that gave views of the middle school's central courtyard and the playground, respectively. On both sides there were trees. In one corner there was a large round table. At the front of the room there was a large green chalkboard; at the rear there was a row of wooden lockers. The desks were low, sized for fourth-graders. On the walls there were instructional cards that showed the proper way to form letters.

What Tricia's teacher had noticed first was that her young student lately seemed always distracted. Her attention span had become noticeably shorter, and as a result, her grades had gone down dramatically—which was why she had asked Tricia to stay after class before they both went on to lunch.

She shut the door and suggested to Tricia that they sit at the table. Tricia sat on the edge of her chair, her legs stretched out straight to the floor.

"Tricia," the young woman began, "is what we're doing in class too hard for you? Are you having trouble keeping up?"

Tricia shook her head no, but even then it seemed she was distracted, *not really listening, toying with the crayons on the table, looking everywhere but at her.*

"You know you can ask me for help."

Tricia nodded.

There was something else, too, almost a weight, some deep lack of joy.

"Is everything all right at home?"

Tricia nodded again, and her teacher, uncertain what else to ask, began a mild warning about the need for her to pay attention in class.

But Tricia wasn't listening, not really, it was obvious. Something else was very much on her mind.

"My daddy plays with my pooty," she blurted out suddenly, leaning back in her chair, looking around.

The young teacher felt more than understood what Tricia had said. She felt a dread in her stomach.

"What's a pooty?" she asked.

Tricia put both her hands between her legs and leaned forward over them, smiling brightly, as if they were playing a game.

"You know."

Her teacher had read all the recent statistics in Newsweek. *She knew what was claimed, that one in four little girls and one in seven little boys were sexually abused; but she wasn't ready for this, not among* her *students, not ready at all.*

"What else does he do?" she asked.

"He makes me play with his pee-pee," Tricia replied, looking off again, her hands still between her legs, clutching herself.

Dear God, the teacher thought, resisting the urge to reach out to touch her, not immediately knowing what she should do, having no notion whatsoever of the nightmare she was about to enter.

5

*I*n southern Mississippi, Sue Hathorn has been invited to address an audience made up of junior high school and high school teachers and counselors. It is one of a hundred or so speeches she makes a year. On the way to the school, she stops at a nearby fast-food restaurant and is sick, nervous, as always, before she gives a talk.

The gymnasium in which she speaks is lit by pale purple mercury vapor lights. On the wall is a huge image of a man who could be Davy Crockett, the manifestation of the spirit by which the school is, presumably, moved: they are known as the Pioneers. Above the image of the man in the buckskin suit is written a quote attributed to Theodore Roosevelt.

It is only through labor
  and prayerful effort
by grim energy
  and absolute courage
that we move on
  to better things.

The three hundred teachers and counselors sit in the bleach ers. The podium is on the hardwood floor of the basketball court.

For the occasion, Sue Hathorn has worn a gray blazer, white blouse, black skirt, and black shoes. Black earrings stand out against her iron-gray hair. Before she begins, she puts on black half-frame reading glasses. She uses her hands as she speaks and looks over the glasses at her audience, making eye contact. Although her words are soft, rounded by soft southern vowels, her voice is firm and confident. She is the very image of everyone's grandmother. She does not stutter, hesitate, or say "Umm," not once.

After a brief introduction by the school's principal, she steps right up and begins, "How many of you—raise your hand now and I'll invite you up here to this podium—how many of you are willing to describe in intimate detail your last sexual experience?"

She raises her own hand, waving it, setting an example, not volunteering.

"How many of you, in front of strangers, are willing to relate exactly what happened, to name the parts, show the motions, name the places?"

Her hand still in the air, she looks around, not challenging the audience but seemingly genuinely curious. She has the teachers' and the counselors' absolute, undivided attention. Overhead, the hum from the purple lights suddenly seems very loud. When no hands appear, she goes on.

"Because when a child is sexually abused, that's exactly what we expect *them* to do. We expect them to tell the welfare workers, the doctors, the policemen, the district attorneys and assistant district attorneys, the judge, a jury. In some cases—I've seen this myself—they are interviewed as many as seventeen times before they even get into a court. *Seventeen times.* And each time they have to relate what none of us adults here want to even once. We ask that of children. *We* do. Our system."

Sue Hathorn pauses, and a glance at the audience reveals a rapt attention, an attention of the sort usually reserved for the borderline incredible, the magician sawing his assistant in half or the televised reports from the front lines of a new war. They are seeing it and they are hearing it but they can't quite believe it, this earnest, grandmotherly type talking about sex, and not just that, about sex with children.

Sue Hathorn reads the audience, carefully gauging the point at which she will lose them. She doesn't want to allow them to file away what she is saying in the "I can't believe that" corner of their minds. She backs off just in time, explaining that she is just like them. At first, she couldn't believe it herself. Then she goes on to talk about her background, how she came to be where she is, doing what she does, a self-made child advocate without real title or portfolio. Just someone who cares. And while in one way that works, giving those teachers and counselors something to hold on to, shared experiences they do understand, life in small towns, high school and college, jobs, marriage, children; in another way it doesn't work at all because in the time allotted she isn't able to explain the why of it: why this pleasant-looking, apparently normal middle-aged woman is discussing from her own firsthand knowledge, not the activities of her bridge or garden club or the forthcoming events at her church, but children's torn vaginas and prolapsed rectums and venereal disease. It just doesn't make sense. It's so distasteful, so ugly, why does she do it at all?

Sue Hathorn was born Betty Sue Gaddy on September 3, 1936, in Copiah County, Mississippi. She has two sisters, one older and one younger. Her father was a farmer who grew cabbages, beans, and tomatoes, scratching out a living in Depression-era southwestern Mississippi. Later on, he would drive a truck and survey land. His daughters were not aware of how little they had because just about everyone around them was in the same shape, working hard, working the land just to get by. Fifty years later, their middle daughter would describe her parents as "the best-est two people I knew."

In the Crystal Springs High School yearbook of 1954, Betty Sue Gaddy appears as both Football Queen and head cheerleader. She was also active on the yearbook staff and in student government. Just as that yearbook gives a certain sense of time and place—the boys with their short buzz-cut or plastered-down hair, their neatly pressed shirts; the girls in full skirts and white socks, blouses buttoned all the way up to the top; the building itself, austere and blocky, stern and reproving, indistinguishable from a hundred other rural high school buildings just like it—it also gives a certain sense of the students individually, of who they were and what they were like. In one picture in particular, posed in the formal dress her mother had made for her, even then, it seems, Betty Sue Gaddy was taking a hard look at the future, looking at it rather than at the camera, not wistful as might be expected but calm and determined and practical.

Predictably enough for a cheerleader, throughout high school Betty Sue Gaddy dated a member of the football team. After graduation, they were engaged to be married. When her fiancé went off to serve in Korea, she waited two years for him, moving to Jackson to work while he was gone, then returning to Copiah County when he came home, setting a date for the wedding. On Saturday nights, they watched *Gunsmoke* and *Have Gun Will Travel* at her parents' house. Her life was on track, going exactly according to plan. Then on November 2, 1957, the plan changed.

That day, Betty Sue and her fiancé had gone to Jackson to pick up the bridesmaids' dresses for the wedding. It had been a full day, and that night, rather than watch TV, she just ate dinner and went to bed. Around midnight, she woke up with the unsettling sense that something was wrong. A short while later, when a car's headlights flashed on the window by her bed, turning into the driveway, she knew her fiancé was dead. She knew it even before his brother reported it to her a few minutes later. He had gone to see his best man. On the way home there had been fog. His car had slipped off the highway, and he had been drowned in a creek. Betty Sue was twenty-one years old, and she lost the next three months of her life. She just doesn't remember them. She knows she kept on at work. She knows that at night she would just go out and drive, but beyond that she doesn't know what happened during that time; and while in subsequent years Betty Sue became just Sue and she met and married another man and changed Gaddy to Hathorn and finally found peace, still she always feels that there is something missing. The loss doesn't hurt anymore, but it is always there, a part of her. In a strange way, she is not afraid of losing again, because that one time she lost all that mattered to her. And she survived.

"You have to experience a bad hurt to really understand it," she says, "what it can do, how it can affect you."

But it took another bad hurt to put her in motion and yet another to make her realize you didn't always have to just take it—sometimes, you can strike back.

After graduating from Crystal Springs High School, Sue Hathorn found a job as a secretary with Mississippi Power and Light, a job she held on to for the next seventeen years, through her fiancé's absence and then his death, through her marriage to Gary Hathorn and his graduation from college and certification as an architect, through their move to Jackson and right up to the time of her mother's death.

For her whole life, Sue Hathorn's mother had been her best friend as well as her mother, her confidante, her mentor; so when she became ill with, among other things, crippling arthritis, it was only natural to Sue to go home to Crystal Springs to visit on weekends. They spoke on the phone every day. While the arthritis was getting much worse, pulling her mother into a knot, still it seemed that, all things considered, she was doing reasonably well. Then one day in the summer of 1971, both because she perceived her illness to be hurting her family and to escape from the severe, chronic pain, her mother took her own life. For Sue Hathorn, another void opened up, though this one carried with it a message, because, while she had not seen it coming, looking back she could see that all the signs had been there. She could see the pain, the desperation, not in what her mother had said every day, but in, finally, what she had done. Once learned, that was a lesson she would not forget. Less than two weeks later, a woman at the First Baptist Church asked Sue if she would let a fifteen-year-old girl from the Youth Court Detention Center sit with her during their prayer meetings on Wednesday nights. Behind the girl's surly belligerence, right away Sue saw her pain.

The girl's name was Jackie. Both Jackie's parents were dead. For a while she had lived at the Baptist Children's Village, but she'd had some adjustment problems there and had ended up in detention—not because she had committed a crime but because there was no other place to put her. Jackie had to walk six miles to school every morning, regardless of the weather; every evening she had to walk back. At night, she was locked in a cell.

"Who wouldn't have chips on their shoulders?" Sue asked herself. "Why can't we take her?" she asked her husband.

Gary Hathorn both was and is easygoing, soft-spoken when he speaks at all, a quiet man not prone to hasty decisions.

"Let her visit on weekends," he said, "and we'll see."

And that's just what they did.

On weekends Sue would pick up Jackie and take her with her to visit her own father—without his wife, the man didn't even know where to find his socks. Not long after that, Gary agreed that they should take Jackie, though with one stipulation: if they took in the child, Sue should quit work to devote herself full-time to being a parent. So Sue quit the job she had had for seventeen years. In her estimation, it was time to move on anyway. At Mississippi Power and Light women weren't considered supervisory material. She was already the secretary to the vice president. The only move up left for her was to be the secretary to the president, which did not seem nearly as important as her child. During the day, while Jackie was at school, Sue went back to school herself and studied psychology. After that Gary and Sue took in two more children, Jerry and Soula. Once Sue saw the need, just how many children needed homes, a modicum of dignity, nurturing, she began to be curious about it, just where all those children came from, so she began to sit in on the Youth Court proceedings—which was when her real education began.

More than anything else, what the Youth Court showed her was how the juvenile courts cycle children through, more or less putting them on hold until they found their way into the penal system. So when she heard about the "Scared Straight" program it seemed only natural to begin that program in Mississippi, to take kids up to the state prison to show them what awaited them if they couldn't find their own track and stay on it. Once a week, she took eight children up to the prison, where for one day they were treated as inmates, actually put behind bars. In each unit, Sue picked out the block leader—the biggest or the baddest—and made sure he got cigarettes or magazines or candy, whatever he wanted, so he would look out for the kids. And while that program did, at times, seem to work, what disturbed her most was that the inmates knew instinctively which of the kids would be back, which of them were their brothers. They would tell her—and all too often they were right. She knew, too, that the state prison terrified her in a way she had never before known. She saw what it meant when a man was dead in his eyes. She knew there had to be a better way to have some effect, to intervene rather than to rectify, but it took her a while to find it.

In Arkansas there was a program called SCAN (Suspected Child Abuse and Neglect). That program centered on a parent aide, a person who could teach another about how to be a parent. Sue decided to start such a program in Mississippi, and she did, though at the same time she continued to work at the Youth Court. What kept her going was the obvious need, the children coming in day after day with cigarette burns and suspiciously broken bones and massive bruises, asking please, could they have a place to stay? Whenever she felt her energy flagging, she would concentrate on one child, one situation, one set of needs, though from that time one case in particular stands out in her mind, a boy of seventeen, handsome, fair-skinned, and polite, a boy who came into the Youth Court late one Friday afternoon to make a complaint. It was just before the weekend, and almost everyone had already gone home.

"I left a beer can in my daddy's car," the boy reported, "and he beat me."

"What do you call a beating?" Sue asked, cynical now, knowing at least some of the scams of which juveniles were capable, knowing enough to begin with some questions. "I mean, a beating might mean one thing to me and another to you."

"I can show you," the boy offered.

Sue nodded, and very soon she knew it was going to be bad, because, even though it was summer, hot as blazes, the boy began to pull off one shirt after another. At the third layer, the blood began to show through. By the time he was down to what was left of his skin, Sue Hathorn was too shocked to speak. All she could think of was the old movies about sailing ships, when they tied sailors to the mast and flogged them. But this wasn't a movie. This was real. The boy's skin had been flayed in strips from his back.

"You wait here," she said, and went to get a court supervisor.

She found a supervisor, all right, and the conversation that followed was one she will never forget.

The supervisor had already left for the weekend, but she paged him and called him back. Already annoyed by her call, more annoyed still that he had to return to the work he had just left, the supervisor did not seem very impressed with the injuries to the boy's back.

"Now, look, son," he offered by way of advice, "you don't have but a year left that you have to stay home. The best thing would be to stick it out. It's not that much longer before you can be out on your own."

Sue was so stunned she very nearly fell out of her chair.

Not knowing what else to do, the boy did, in fact, return to his parents' home.

The lesson took a while to sink in.

Sue Hathorn did not know then what she could have done, not with an officer of the court telling her there was nothing they *could* do, but she knew that there *had* to be something. She was right, of course, there *was* something, but until her own attitude changed she would not know what that something was, not for that one boy, not for all the other children just like him.

"I will never allow that to happen again," she swore to herself. "I will never *not* know what to do. There is always something that can be done, and I will get help for that child. *I will get help for that child.*"

What Sue Hathorn had learned was the propelling power of her own anger, an undercurrent not lost on her audience of counselors and teachers in that high school auditorium as she continues her speech.

"'To be a victim at the hands of the criminal,'" she goes on, her words still soft but confident, earnest and compelling, "'is an unforgettable nightmare. But to then become a victim at the hands of the criminal justice system is an unforgivable travesty. It makes the criminal and the criminal justice system partners in crime.'" She takes off her glasses and allows them to dangle from the cord around her neck. "That's a quote from a man named Robert Grayson. And you know, when I first read it, I didn't know what he meant by that. What does that mean anyway—that the criminal and the criminal justice system are partners in crime?"

Again, her eyes search the audience, as if looking for an answer herself. She puts her glasses back on.

"What I'll do, I'll let a child tell you what that means. I'll read you a letter she wrote to her teacher."

Sue Hathorn puts one hand in the pocket of her skirt. Although she is reciting from memory, with her other hand she picks up a piece of paper from the podium, as if she were reading the letter itself.

" 'I asked you for help,' " she begins, " 'and you told me you would help me if I told you the things my parents did to me. It was very hard for me to say all those things, but you told me to trust you. Then you made me repeat those things to fourteen different strangers.

" 'I asked you for privacy, and you sent two policemen to my school who in front of everyone made me "go downtown."

" 'I asked you to believe me, and you said that you did; then I was questioned by lawyers and doctors and policemen.

" 'I asked you to help me, and you gave me that doctor with the cold hands and cold instruments, just like my parents. He told me not to cry, just like my parents. He said I looked fine, which was good news for me, but bad news for my case.

" 'I asked you to keep quiet, and you told the newspapers. What does it matter that they left out my name? They used my parents' name and my home address.

" 'I asked you for protection, and you gave me a social worker who patted my head and called me "honey." Mostly because she couldn't remember my name. She sent me to live with strangers in another place, with a different school. Do you know what it's like to live where there is a lock on the refrigerator? Do you know what it's like to live where you have to ask permission to use the shampoo and the hair dryer? Do you know what it's like to have more social workers than friends? To have your sister hate you and your brother call you a liar? It's my word against my parents' word. I'm twelve years old. My father is the manager of the bank.' "

Sue Hathorn pauses, glancing up, again looking around.

" 'You forced my mother to choose between me and my father. She chose my father. She was scared. She had a lot to lose.' "

Sue Hathorn carefully puts the page she was holding on the podium, placing it face down.

" 'I had a lot to lose, too—the difference was, you never told me how much.' "

Just for a moment, in Sue Hathorn's eyes Betty Sue Gaddy is there, the cheerleader, the survivor of deep hurt and loss.

"There is always something we can do, people. There is *always* something we can do."

It is the creed she lives by, so honestly expressed that even before she steps away from the podium, even before the applause from the teachers and counselors begins, Sue Hathorn is reminding herself of what *she* has to do next. She had read in the newspaper that evidence about Bingo Depot would be presented to the next session of the Hinds County grand jury. If she wanted a piece of that bingo-money pie, she knew she'd better talk to Robert Malone, show some support, before he went out and got himself indicted.

6

Robert Malone is talking about himself. At the wheel of his full-size, extended-cab Chevrolet pickup truck, he appears relaxed, driving with one hand, not going unduly fast but hardly stopping either, rolling through stop signs and around any vehicles that get in his way. The truck's interior is plush, not like a truck at all, outfitted with an array of gauges, bucket seats, a fancy stereo, a telephone mounted on the dash. On his belt he wears a beeper. When the beeper sounds, he punches out a number on the phone, then speaks into the microphone affixed to the sun visor. There are flecks of gray in his dark brown hair that just covers the tops of his ears and falls just over his collar. There is about him a certain energy, a quickness of comprehension and eye movement. Today he is wearing his contact lenses. His eyes are very hard and very blue, made to seem even bluer by the dark lids that frame them.

"I went to meet this guy because I wanted to buy Bingo Depot. This guy, he was being run out of town by the Attorney General. He'd gotten a room over at the Howard Johnson's, and the first thing he did when I got there was to tell me to take off my clothes."

His beeper sounds.

Robert Malone listens to the message, decides not to return the call.

"He wanted to make sure I wasn't wearing a wire."

Robert Malone lights a filtered cigarette from a gold pack, one of fifty or so cigarettes he will smoke that day.

"So I strip. He looks me over, and that's how I bought the Depot, sitting there bare-assed naked."

It is exactly the sort of story Robert Malone relishes telling. It touches on a shadowy world, the "gray area," he calls it, of activities and people on the edge of the law, of machines that are legal to own but illegal to use, games that can or cannot be played legally, depending upon who is doing the playing.

"After a while," he adds, "he got tired of looking at my naked ass, so he gave me a towel."

He pronounces "naked" as *nekked*. He rolls out around a car halted at a stop sign, turns left from the left-hand lane.

"What the Attorney General had done to this guy was to raid him for selling pull-tabs, gambling cards, sort of like an instant lottery. They threw in operating an illegal bingo hall, too. They confiscated all his equipment. What they told him was, you either forfeit all your equipment and all your money and sign an agreement saying you won't ever come back into Mississippi for two years or we're going to charge you with racketeering, too. So he gave it up and left. It was a financial decision. He knew his legal fees would eat him up—he was from out of state and didn't much care anyway."

Robert Malone gives a halfhearted shrug.

"Attorney fees are a part of the business, an expense, like light bulbs."

His beeper sounds again, but this time he returns the call, using the handset, keeping the conversation private rather than speaking into the microphone on the sun visor. After a brief interchange, he picks up exactly where he left off.

"So what I did, before I even started a bingo game, I had Mike Farrell meet with people from the Attorney General's

Office. I wanted to get it straight, how to keep it legal. Me and Mike Farrell, we met with John Kitchens, an attorney from the Attorney General's Office, and Hal Ratchford, an investigator from the Attorney General's Office. After that, they'd call me up and ask me about other bingo games, whether or not they was legal. They'd ask *me*, you understand? Well, the Attorney General had already issued at least two opinions that I know of that bingo was legal, one to the chief of police of Meridian and one to the city of Natchez. Now we're getting down close to it. You listening carefully?"

Robert Malone exhales smoke through his nose, mashes out his cigarette in the ashtray so hard the dashboard rattles.

"See, before he was elected Attorney General, Mike Moore was a bad-ass district attorney down on the coast. A kick-ass-on-crime type of guy. Well, I supplied every bingo hall in Jackson County the whole time he was district attorney. That was before bingo was legal. Bingo was illegal. Dead-ass illegal. No exceptions to the law before the statute was passed in 1987. But bingo had been in operation for thirty years. When Mike Moore was district attorney in Pascagoula, there were ten bingo halls going the whole time. What I'm saying is, he was not too fucking concerned with the law then. There wasn't even a statutory exemption then, not for a charity, not for anything. So why is he concerned with the constitution now? He didn't have a problem with bingo when he was going to a Catholic school that was funded by bingo. He didn't have a problem with bingo when his mother was playing it. And even since he's been Attorney General he's issued two opinions that bingo is legal. So now this lottery thing comes around. There's big money on the table—I mean, *big* money—and all of a sudden Mike Moore is concerned about bingo. *Now* it's a lottery."

Robert Malone's eyes take on a dark cast.

"Now ain't that just the biggest fucking coincidence?"

7

O̶n her way home from work, Dana Gardner has stopped by to see Sue Hathorn, ostensibly to ask her advice but really just to blow off steam. Dana Gardner is a caseworker for the Mississippi Department of Child Protective Services. She looks upon Sue Hathorn as a mentor, a calming influence, someone to turn to who will, at least, understand. As with virtually every one of the workers in her office, Dana Gardner's case load is astounding. Twenty cases would, perhaps, be workable. Thirty cases per worker is the national average. Yet in recent weeks Dana Gardner's case load has topped *two hundred*. Burdened by that overwhelming work load, she has by necessity become more of a case manager than a social worker. She investigates and diagnoses situations and writes up prescriptions for possible remedies, then spends far too much time on the phone trying to get her clients into the excruciatingly limited programs and services. She is unable, she readily admits, to spend nearly enough time with families.

"You should have seen where I went this morning," Dana Gardner says. Her voice is high and childlike, singsong. She is the mother of two young children herself, in her late twenties, very pretty, with brown hair that comes down past her shoulders. Despite her on-the-job experiences, she seems unaffected by the horrors, still enthusiastic, wide-eyed in her innocence.

"The house was over there." She gives a limp-wristed wave at the wall—it doesn't really matter where the house is. "The grandmother called. The mother is a crackhead. She comes and goes. The girl is fourteen. Somehow she got herself pregnant." Dana Gardner laughs at herself, a giggly laugh that does not interrupt the high-speed flow of her words. "Well, I guess I know *how* she got herself pregnant. Anyway, the mother finds out. She's all cracked out, says the girl has ruined the family honor. She punches her in the stomach. The girl falls down, and the mother starts kicking her, kicking her in the stomach— kicked her all the way across the kitchen floor. The grandmother saw the whole thing."

"Good," Sue Hathorn interjects, acknowledging the value of having a witness.

"The grandmother got her to a hospital. The girl miscarried. There'll be a physician's report."

"What about the child?"

"She's all right where she is, at her grandmother's." Dana shrugs. "She's still in school. I wrote it up, called the police. The mother will go down for a few years. The girl will be out on her own by then."

"Maybe," Sue Hathorn warns.

"Maybe," Dana Gardner agrees. With two hundred other cases to juggle, there is a certain mercy in this one, the semblance of a resolution, of having been able to help. "I spent the rest of the morning in court."

"Whose court?"

"Henley's." Dana Gardner laughs again. "Can't you guess? Why do you think I have on this blouse?" She pinches a piece of the blouse's almost sheer material, pulling it away from her shoulder. "This afternoon I had a removal. The parents are furious."

For all its faults, Mississippi's child protective system is very good at identifying homes where a child is at risk. Social workers have enormous power. The course of events that leads to the removal of a child from a home—or the return of a child to a home—begins with them; the *problems* begin with what comes next. There are inadequate facilities for children who *have* been removed. There is not enough money for therapists, for foster care, for guardians *ad litem*, attorneys who protect the children's rights. There is no money for parent-aide programs or family coordinators or crisis day care. And, of course, there are far too few caseworkers.

"I got Henley on the phone to okay the order for removal. I had to get him at home. Can you believe? Three o'clock and he was already gone."

Sue Hathorn can believe it.

"Do you remember that little girl I had? The one who was so hungry she ate the head off the mop?"

Sue Hathorn nods, easily following Dana Gardner's quick shift to another case. It is a way of thinking they share, an adaptive mechanism, the ability to skip from one thought or case to another, like a television scanning through channels, because any one program, any one case dwelled on too long could readily lead to despair.

"She's going home tomorrow."

Sue Hathorn's look seems to question the wisdom of that.

Dana Gardner shrugs.

"The mother completed the parenting class, took the bus and made it there eight weeks in a row."

Dana Gardner suddenly jerks herself up straight, as if she had come in contact with a mild electric current. She glances at the clock on the wall and hurriedly gets up to leave.

"I better get myself home before my children call in and report *me*."

Sue Hathorn stands up and gives Dana Gardner a hug.

"Take care of yourself, my dear. Call me if you need anything."

Dana Gardner rummages through her huge purse, looking for her keys.

"Sue, you better get us some money. We're drowning out here."

"I'm working on it," Sue Hathorn replies. "Meantime, save your cans."

She gestures toward the big sack of aluminum cans in the corner.

Dana Gardner does not reply to that but finds her keys and holds them in one hand, a reminder that she does, indeed, have them. For a moment, she stands stock-still.

"Do you think Lucas and Philip would eat pizza again for dinner?" she asks vaguely, obviously weighing the possibility, now really done with work, thinking of getting on home.

8

It had been explained to her, what was happening, by the lady who had come to school to talk to her, but that didn't mean that she understood it. She knew what she had done must have been very wrong, to tell the secret, because now it seemed she was being punished, just like her father had told her she would be if she told.

The girl in the bed next to her wailed horribly, more than a nightmare, a night terror. She was afraid that she had lost everything. She was just plain afraid.

But at least he would not come into her room that night. At least she had that.

They had promised.

She covered her ears and tried not to listen, weighing one thing against the other, considering things no nine-year-old should have to consider.

Along about downtown, the difference between Jackson and South Jackson becomes visibly apparent. The cars change from new Hondas and BMWs to old Chevys and Fords. There are a lot of well-worn pickup trucks. Somewhere along in there, too, the theme of the bars changes from stained glass and hanging plants to country. South Jackson is the poor part of town, the other side of the tracks, where the lack of money becomes obvious. There are homes and businesses and industrial works all in close proximity. There are housing projects rather than apartment complexes. There is trash on the streets. Through downtown and on out, the road leads to a quiet neighborhood, an almost hidden residential area that has seen better days. This day is gray and blustery, a bleak day.

The house itself is small and wood-frame, modest, low, sort of ranch-style, with nothing there, really, to distinguish it from the other houses in the area. Inside, the changes to the house are apparent, but it takes a few moments to understand what those changes are. The big center hall doubles as the dining area. There are only two bedrooms, but there are far too many beds— and far too many children for a one-family home. There is a small kitchen, a large laundry room with an industrial-strength washer and dryer, an office in the front room that probably had been intended as a living area, perhaps a place to greet people before taking them on into the home. And it is just that now, though the office comes as a bit of a surprise, not exactly what the builder had envisioned when he conceived of greeting people at the front door.

This is the only emergency shelter for children aged birth through twelve years in Hinds County, the county in which the city of Jackson is located, a country with a population of over a quarter of a million.

The shelter is funded through the Department of Human Services, the United Way, a sponsoring church, and private contributions—in other words, they scramble after money wherever they can find it.

"Money is the critical issue," the director, Janice Wilder, says candidly. "It gets down to whether or not we can pay the rent and the utilities and the water."

The paint is peeling in places, and the plaster is cracked. The two sleeping areas are segregated only by sex. Three-month-old infants and twelve-year-old near adolescents and every age in between sleep in close proximity, side by side. Behind the smell of strong disinfectant the overworked house is shot through with the smell of dirty diapers and food odors and dust. There simply are too many children in too little space, and virtually every one of them has left behind all that they have previously known—their brothers and sisters, their own bedrooms, their favorite toys. Some of them have been so traumatized that they have severe behavioral problems. They are violent. They steal. They try to abuse the other children, striking back. Sometimes, the parents find out where the shelter is: it has been entered at gunpoint and threatened with bombs. There are heavy locks on the doors and there are bars on the windows.

This is the place Tricia Alexander is staying, covering her ears, trying not to hear the wail of the night terrors, this because at nine years of age she has been repeatedly raped, this her first night in the care of the best the state has to offer.

9

On the side opposite downtown from the shelter, about five minutes from the state capitol, just before the entrance to I-55, is the Jackson Square Bar and Grill. Because it is convenient to, yet slightly removed from, the capitol and the other government buildings that surround it, the restaurant is popular with politicians and others in government or government-related service who have an hour or two for lunch.

The building is set into the side of a hill, almost adobelike in its massing. It is a relatively new building, upscale, gray with white trim. The parking lot is made from that black and seamless sort of asphalt, and the stripes are freshly painted, white and crisp, delineating the spaces for the American sedans, the Mercedes-Benzes, and the Japanese luxury cars that seem to be the vehicles of choice.

Inside, the walls are light gray. In the front room, where you are likely to be seated if the management knows you, there is gray brick trim and a dark wood ceiling. In the rear room, where everyone else goes, areas are partitioned by sheets of stainless steel cut through with various designs. There are the almost-requisite plants with long, creeping branches, and Italian sconces are on the wall. The booths are dark green. The tables are set with linen napkins and candles. Without a single exception, the men wear coats and ties. The women are dressed up for lunch in fashionable dresses and suits, makeup and hair fresh. The menu is impressive. The salad dressings have names you cannot possibly interpret unless they have already been explained to you. There is lively chatter, hearty good humor, earnest talk, a constant hum—at least some of the wheels of government in motion.

On any given workday, Mike Moore is likely to eat lunch here at the Jackson Square Bar and Grill. It is convenient to his office in the Carroll Gartin Justice Building. The food is good, if a little overpriced. Why not? He deserves it. No one questions that he has worked hard to get where he is, the youngest chief legal officer in the history of the state.

After graduation from law school at Ole Miss, uncertain what, exactly, he wanted to do with his hard-won law degree, Mike Moore went home to Pascagoula and opened his own small practice. He did some public defender work and after a few months of that was offered a job as a part-time assistant district attorney, which he readily accepted. As an ADA he got to try cases, and he found that he was good at it. He enjoyed it. He was twenty-four years old. Two years later, when the district attorney got elected to another office, Mike Moore decided to run for district attorney himself. He ran on a clean-up-government campaign, and to the surprise of many, he won; and to their further surprise, he *did* clean up local government. Among other things, he indicted on corruption charges four of the five county supervisors, powerful, entrenched, old-line politicians, a move most people thought was going to get him killed—and there *were* threats.

"It was intense," he recalls. "I had all sorts of threats, but the job needed to be done."

And he worked at it and he was successful and his popularity soared.

During his terms as district attorney, he also aggressively

prosecuted child abuse cases. If you ask him about that time and those cases, he will tell you, "Talk to Cathy Meeks." Catherine Meeks is a well-known and respected psychologist who specializes in working with children. She knew him and worked with him when he was on the coast and now, as he does, lives in Jackson. "She lives just two houses down from me," he will add. Catherine Meeks also went to Ole Miss, and she and Mike Moore are only six months apart in age.

"His reputation was of giving priority to child abuse cases and trying them vigorously, and the times I was in court with him he seemed to do that."

Cathy Meeks is tall and very attractive, with dark hair framing a long face. Her eyes are at the same time gentle and probing, alert. Her voice is low, almost soothing.

"He would argue vociferously before the jury. He would take into consideration the needs of the child. He did a good job. It seemed to be a priority with him. And I think that was partly because there were people around him who were pressuring him and feeding him information and trying to push him to make this a priority and he listened to them. I think he really did."

And with all that behind him, with his experience as an assistant district attorney and his success as a district attorney, about ten years of hard work, Mike Moore decided to run for state Attorney General because, as he saw it, "I'd done everything that a district attorney can do."

On the wall of his office, framed, he keeps the necktie he wore often during that campaign. The tie is frayed and worn and spotted with rain and mud and grease and sweat, a reminder of all the hard work, the long hours.

"I ran," he recalls, "and I used what I'd already done before."

"I think toward the end of his tenure as DA, though," Cathy Meeks goes on, "he was more interested in the Attorney General's race. The last case that I worked on out of his office, he was supposed to try the case and he handed it off to an assistant district attorney and the case was lost and he was nowhere to be found."

There is in her voice a resignation that makes it hard not to recall that old photograph of the new state capitol, an understanding of the way things work. It is, perhaps, why Mike Moore specifically uses her as a reference, a psychologist, a doctor, someone certified in the science of mind and behavior.

"See, I mean I'm not even too much disappointed in Mike Moore," Cathy Meeks goes on, talking about the years since Mike Moore became Attorney General, "because I never had an expectation that it would be any different than this. He's a politician, and I understand that. And politicians live and exist for one thing: to get votes and get elected and climb the political ladder. And they do whatever is expedient to further that cause, and when they give lip service to 'this is an issue that is important to me,' I know—and I don't even hold this against them—I just know that this is true, that the reason they're doing that is because it's politically expedient. And when it's no longer politically expedient to say that, they don't say it anymore. That's the nature of the beast. That's who he is. I never expected it to be any different. When I say I'm not disappointed, what I mean is, I never had any illusions that it would be any different. When I say I don't hold it against him, it's like I never idealized him to begin with."

The emergency shelter in South Jackson seems a part of another, alien world, the memory of it seeming to come from another dimension as you leave the Jackson Square Bar and Grill with the taste still in your mouth of yellow-fin tuna with a fancy sauce and a salad with a fancy dressing.

10

*W*hat Sue Hathorn did in the weeks following the raid on Bingo Depot was to call Robert Malone regularly, to drop by to see him whenever she could, at the same time that she tried to check him out. It was disconcerting to her to have her calls returned from various pay phones, the background noises different each time, or when they met to have him put his finger to his lips, indicating that she should not speak; but even that was not nearly so disconcerting as when she considered what might have happened if she had been up on that stage in Bingo Depot, accepting money, when the police had conducted their raid. One of her own first rules of dealing with abused children was, never promise what you cannot deliver. And there was good reason for that: those children most times had been lied to and deceived so often that, if any healing was to begin, they had to know that they could expect the truth from at least one person. No matter how badly you wanted to say, "It's going to be okay, you'll be all right," you couldn't say it—not even that—because more times than not it was not going to be okay. They were not going to be all right. More significantly, what you *could* do was to honestly explain as best you could the various situations, and when you gave your word, you kept it. That creed was not hers alone but extended to all those genuinely concerned for the children. If her credibility was tarnished in any way, if her reputation was even remotely suspect, she would lose the support of other professionals in the field. She would lose her good name, the basis on which she solicited donations, and what was worst of all, she would lose the respect of the children and so her own self-respect, because in Sue Hathorn the one thing was very much intertwined with the other. Still, after all those years of soliciting donations, processing grant applications, collecting aluminum cans, for the first time she saw the potential for regular financial support. She allowed herself to dream of what might be accomplished, a Children's Advocacy Center, legal aid for children, lobbying for new laws at the state and even the national level. She did not worry at all about whether she could persuade Robert Malone to take her on as "his" charity. What it came down to was, could she trust him?

She didn't know. She didn't know him well enough to decide, but the more she thought about it, the more she convinced herself that she had to take the chance. Normally, she might have gone to her church for guidance, but in this instance that was not an option: like almost one in four people in the state of Mississippi, Sue Hathorn is a Baptist, and she knew the Baptists frowned on gambling in any form, even bingo. She even agreed that they had a point, too, that what gambling did was to make the majority losers so that a few could be winners. Hardly righteous. The temptation, of course, was to say that she didn't care where the money came from, but the fact was, she did. There were limits. What if, for example, a child pornography business offered her a large contribution? Could she accept that? Of course not. Because the purpose then would be maintenance, maintaining the children to suffer more abuse. That was why there was child advocacy in the first place, because without it all the rest—the intervention, the therapy, the medical treatment— was pernicious. Help children, keep them healthy, so that they could suffer more abuse? But did *bingo* really threaten the children? So okay, gambling *did* make losers, no doubt about it, and bingo *was* gambling, no doubt about that either; but she could make sure the *children* were ultimately the winners. And wasn't that her own motto? The bumper sticker on her car? "*Children first.*" She was supposed to know who she was—heck, she was old enough. When had *she* begun to worry about what other people thought of her? She knew well enough that they were going to think what they wanted anyway.

Finally, the decision seemed to make itself. Through her calls and her visits, Sue Hathorn began to *like* Robert Malone. Though she was not unaware of the tricks the mind could play, how the wish could shape the rationale, she began to believe he was innocent, that he was caught in a political cross fire—from her own experience with the children, she was skeptical of the legal system anyway, knowing full well how it could be abused. But finally, she saw the way to get the money to really help. All she had to do was to have the strength to persevere, to stand by him and convince him to take up her cause even as the state Attorney General was calling him a gangster and a thief. She was playing a hunch, and she knew it, gambling herself. All she had to risk was her status within her church and her credibility within her profession. All she had to wager was her good name, the good work she had done for close to twenty years, the respect of others and her own self-respect.

All she needed was courage.

For his part, Robert Malone was not so skeptical of the legal system. He didn't have the time to be. He was too busy fighting for his life.

11

*R*ight from the beginning, it was complicated. No. 140,677(D2). THE STATE OF MISSISSIPPI, EX REL. MIKE MOORE, ATTORNEY GENERAL, PLAINTIFF, v. ROBERT M. MALONE d/b/a BINGO DEPOT, ET AL., DEFENDANTS. And after that first day in the Chancery Court of the First Judicial District of Hinds County, Mississippi, it did not look good for Robert Malone. Not good at all.

What the state had obtained from the Chancery Court, the Honorable W. O. Dillard, chancellor, was a temporary restraining order without notice. That was the order that had allowed the surprise raid on Bingo Depot, because, Special Assistant Attorney General Jim Warren had sworn, "the State of Mississippi will suffer irreparable injury if notice is given. Specifically, if defendants are given prior notice, then there is a substantial likelihood the defendants, or some of them, will abscond with evidence material to the case." Mike Farrell had come right back with a motion to lift the temporary restraining order. In short order thereafter, within the next week, there would be a dizzying array of other motions: a motion for modification of the temporary restraining order, a motion to continue the motion to cite for contempt and a motion to recuse, a motion to extend the temporary restraining order and the motion for contempt. That first day, January 12, 1990, Robert Malone took the stand himself, a mistake he would not be prone to repeat.

Under questioning by Mike Farrell, his own lawyer, Robert Malone testified that he had met with representatives of the Attorney General's Office to make sure that he was in compliance with the law.

"Our whole reason for the meeting," he stated under oath, "was that we wanted to make sure we were in compliance with what that statute said along with what Mike Moore's opinion was and wanted to be in compliance."

After some discussion of just what compliance was—which was, basically, that all the proceeds of a bingo game had to benefit a charity—Mike Farrell tried to make it clear to the court that his client, and Metro Charities, the charity that supposedly received the proceeds from the games, had made every effort to be cooperative, to be in compliance, and that the temporary restraining order without notice was, therefore, uncalled for.

From the official transcript of that first hearing:

MIKE FARRELL: At the conclusion of the meeting, was there any discussion about books and records?

ROBERT MALONE: We told Mr. Kitchens and Mr. Ratchford that anytime they wanted to see our books or our records, all they had to do was call us or come by, they were welcome to see anything. Any questions they had about anything we did, we would be glad to show them.

MIKE FARRELL: Did they take you up on your offer?

ROBERT MALONE: They have not. They have called before and talked to me before on the phone, but not about Metro Charities.

MIKE FARRELL: Okay. Did you have any conversation with them about Metro Charities' compliance with this Attorney General's opinion?

ROBERT MALONE: At the time we asked them if we were—you know, we told them how everything was done at Metro Charities, and as far as they were concerned, we were in compliance with that. And they voiced no objections to anything we were doing. At the time we had, you know, just taken over operation of Bingo Depot, which had been—and we were trying to make sure that we were not going to have any problems with Bingo Depot, because we wanted to make sure we were in compliance all the way down the line. And that's the reason, to keep controversy from stirring in there, we wanted to let them know that anytime they wanted to see the books it was okay. They did not have to have subpoenas and search warrants and all that; they could just call us. We wanted to cooperate. They've never called me that I've not answered a question they asked.

MIKE FARRELL: Has the Jackson Police Department made a similar request for books and records?

ROBERT MALONE: No, sir. But I also made it available to them anytime they'd like to have it.

MIKE FARRELL: Who did you make it available to?

ROBERT MALONE: I talked at the time—Lieutenant Fitzgerald was chief of Vice and Narcotics. This was a day or so after we met with Mr. Kitchens. I called Mr. Fitzgerald, and, in fact, I met him for lunch to tell him that we, as Metro Charities, had taken, you know, over Bingo Depot and any questions, you know, as to how we did things or so forth, because of the city's, you know, participation, that we would be glad to answer their questions or give them anything they'd like to see. And I told him that we had had a meeting, you know, with Mr. Kitchens and that if either one had any questions, we'd be glad to answer their questions.

MIKE FARRELL: Mr. Malone, do you operate any of the Bingo Depots in your individual capacity?

ROBERT MALONE: No.

MIKE FARRELL: Have you ever told anybody that you did as an individual as opposed to Metro Charities?

ROBERT MALONE: No.

MIKE FARRELL: Were you sued in this action individually?

ROBERT MALONE: Yes.

So far, so good.

Even the Attorney General's special assistant, Jim Warren, remarked, "Quite frankly, I get the impression after listening to you talk that you feel like you've worked real closely with the Attorney General's Office to try to comply." To which Robert Malone replied, "I feel like that we've offered everything that we had." But Jim Warren was about to put matters in quite another light. He began simply enough, with questions about the locations of Robert Malone's for-profit businesses and the location of Metro Charities.

JIM WARREN: What is located at 1601 Handy Avenue?

ROBERT MALONE: 1601 Handy is where Capitol Air Specialists, the air pollution control company, was located at and Malone Sales. They're both in the same building.

JIM WARREN: Okay. Now, are you sure on that address? Are you sure it's 1601 Handy?

ROBERT MALONE: That is where—1601 Handy is where Capitol Air Specialists is; it's where Malone Sales was also located with Capitol Air.

JIM WARREN: Okay.

ROBERT MALONE: Malone Sales has recently moved.

JIM WARREN: And what is its address now?

ROBERT MALONE: 1625 Handy Avenue.

JIM WARREN: Okay. Now, who owns Malone Sales and who owns the other company you referred to?

ROBERT MALONE: Malone Sales is owned by myself. Capitol Air Specialists is in the process—well, it has—the deal has been final. It was bought by United Air Specialists in Cincinnati, Ohio.

JIM WARREN: Are these for-profit or not-for-profit organizations?

ROBERT MALONE: They're both for-profit companies.

JIM WARREN: The complaint you were served with, did it

include a set of the articles of incorporation of Metro Charities, Inc.?

ROBERT MALONE: Yes.

JIM WARREN: It did. Okay. I'm going to hand that to you, after showing it to counsel.

[*Document tendered for review.*]

JIM WARREN: Now, what I'm about to hand you is Exhibit A to the complaint. Can you tell me what that is?

ROBERT MALONE: That's the articles of incorporation for Metro Charities.

JIM WARREN: In other words, that's a copy of those articles?

ROBERT MALONE: Right.

JIM WARREN: Would you look through it and make sure that all the pages are there and all that kind of stuff?

[*Witness reviews document.*]

JIM WARREN: Did you look at the articles of incorporation?

ROBERT MALONE: Yes.

JIM WARREN: Okay. Now, would you pick that back up and read to me the name of the organization that is incorporated there?

ROBERT MALONE: Metro Charities, Incorporated.

JIM WARREN: Is that your not-for-profit corporation?

ROBERT MALONE: Yes.

JIM WARREN: The one that you incorporated?

ROBERT MALONE: Yes.

JIM WARREN: Tell me the address of Metro Charities.

ROBERT MALONE: 1601 Handy.

That curious fact established, that the charity and the for-profit businesses were located at the same address, Jim Warren moved on, circling, making Robert Malone reveal the facts he wanted revealed, until finally he would conclude for the court that the testimony "shed some light on a situation that is not a very pretty one. It's a situation where, under the guise of maintaining a charitable organization, some people are making substantial sums of money, making a lot of money, most of it cash."

Jim Warren: Is it true or is it not true that you've had transactions of that nature and that nature alone that are in excess of seven hundred fifty thousand dollars during that same time period?

Robert Malone: In a year's time period?

Jim Warren: Since February of last year. And think real hard because this is verifiable.

Robert Malone: That's possible.

Jim Warren: Okay. So you're saying it's possible that you've done three-quarters of a million dollars in that account since February last year?

Robert Malone: Uh-huh [*Affirmative*].

Jim Warren: Now, tell me again how much money you gave to charity out of the account.

Robert Malone: Forty to forty-five thousand dollars.

Jim Warren: All right.

Robert Malone: Would you like to know the expenses?

Jim Warren: I know all I need to know.

On the face of it, it was a hard point to rebut: by Robert Malone's own accounting of all that cash, three-quarters of a million dollars had gone into Bingo Depot; forty to forty-five thousand dollars had gone to charity. But Jim Warren did, in fact, want to know about at least some of the expenses Robert Malone had alluded to.

Jim Warren: Now, you're paid a salary or stipend or some amount from Metro Charities. Is that correct?

Robert Malone: Uh-huh [*affirmative*].

Jim Warren: How much are you paid?

Robert Malone: A thousand dollars a week.

Jim Warren: Okay.

Robert Malone: I also pay my own expenses.

Jim Warren: You pay them out of your pocket?

Robert Malone: Right.

Jim Warren: Now, this is not the only business you're in. Am I correct?

ROBERT MALONE: Right.

JIM WARREN: You sell bingo supplies, don't you?

ROBERT MALONE: Yes, sir. I've sold bingo supplies for about ten years.

JIM WARREN: You own that business yourself. That's not owned by Metro Charities. Am I correct?

ROBERT MALONE: Yes, I own it myself.

JIM WARREN: Is it a corporation or is it a sole proprietorship?

ROBERT MALONE: Sole proprietor.

JIM WARREN: Now, how much in sales have you made to Bingo Depot since February? How much stuff have you sold from your business to Bingo Depot and the other two operations that Metro Charities runs?

ROBERT MALONE: In supplies?

JIM WARREN: Yes. Since February of last year. And you can approximate. I understand you don't have it down to the cent.

ROBERT MALONE: Probably eighty to a hundred thousand dollars, somewhere in there.

JIM WARREN: Were those transactions by check or in cash?

ROBERT MALONE: By check.

JIM WARREN: Do you sell your supplies for cost to this organization and then for a profit to others, or do you sell it for a profit to this one, too?

ROBERT MALONE: I sell supplies to Metro Charities cheaper than I sell to anybody else.

JIM WARREN: I asked you—

ROBERT MALONE: And that's below suggested, you know, retail.

JIM WARREN: But do you sell it for cost?

ROBERT MALONE: I don't sell it for cost, no.

JIM WARREN: So you're not in the charity business.

ROBERT MALONE: Malone Sales is not a charity.

JIM WARREN: And Robert Malone is not in the charity business either, is he? You're in it to make money.

ROBERT MALONE: In Metro Charities?

JIM WARREN: You're in the bingo business to make money—

ROBERT MALONE: I'm in the bingo supply business to make money.

JIM WARREN: Okay. But what do you call that fifty-two thousand dollars that Metro Charities pays you a year? Is that money or is it not?

ROBERT MALONE: Yeah, it's a salary. I suppose it is.

JIM WARREN: Okay. So—

ROBERT MALONE: Out of that fifty-two thousand, you can just about chalk up twenty-five or thirty thousand dollars of it for expenses.

JIM WARREN: Okay. And tell me again—

ROBERT MALONE: I put fifty thousand miles a year on my truck.

JIM WARREN: I'm sorry. I didn't mean to interrupt you. Tell me again how much money you gave to charity out of the Jackson operation. Did you give more to charity or less to charity than you made off Metro Charities last year out of the Jackson operation? More or less than fifty-two thousand?

ROBERT MALONE: Than I made off of Metro Charities?

JIM WARREN: Yes.

ROBERT MALONE: I made more gross salary than I gave, yeah.

Of course, there was more to the story. Later, on redirect, Robert Malone was able to account for very nearly all of the $750,000 that Jim Warren had made so much of. Among other things, at Bingo Depot there had been extensive remodeling, new air conditioning, rent of nearly eight thousand dollars a month, and an electric bill that ran from four to seven thousand dollars a month, "depending on how hot it was." The supplies, too, of course, cost a lot of money. But the Honorable W. O. Dillard, chancellor, had heard about enough, and he said so on the record.

THE COURT: There's got to be an end to everything, though, and we're all going to miss supper and miss deer hunting tomorrow and all weekend if we don't limit this.

So at the court's pleasure, closing arguments were heard,

and very quickly it became clear that Robert Malone, despite all the questions, was not the subject of the lawsuit. As Jim Warren, the Attorney General's own special assistant, had stated earlier, not once but twice, the real subject of the lawsuit was Section 97-33-51 of the Mississippi Code, the statute that the state legislature had passed three years earlier that had made bingo legal. And it was exactly to this point that Mike Farrell addressed his closing argument.

MIKE FARRELL: In the Attorney General's Complaint, they state the irreparable harm that the people of Mississippi will suffer is that there will be a constitutional violation, and for that reason, your honor, this constitutional violation, if it exists at all, has been with us a long time—as long as gambling or as long as bingo has been around. The issue came to a head in 1987 when the legislature created an exemption from the gambling statutes for nonprofit charitable organizations that have bingos and raffles. That constitutional question has been here for at least two years. Where is the irreparable injury that was so great that the Attorney General couldn't call the attorney for Robert Malone the day before? What was the urgency? . . . If you look at the Complaint, they don't accuse Mr. Malone of wrongdoing. What they say is, they say the Mississippi legislature is guilty of unlawful activity . . . The Attorney General says the legislature, in giving this exemption to the defendants, acted unlawfully and unconstitutionally. That's the legal question, that's the political question that they want answered in such a hurry . . . They say, Judge, we want you to decide that the legislature created this statute and it's unconstitutional. That's the real defendant in this case, the Mississippi legislature. Why aren't they sitting here instead of Mr. Malone?

Indeed, as the Chancery Court ruled that day and as, eventually, the state Supreme Court would rule, that *was* the question: had the legislature passed a statute that was unconstitutional?

THE COURT: I think it's a pretty clear issue that's been raised, and now it's time for us to deal with it. And maybe everybody would understand the judicial branch of government and the legislative branch of government and the executive branch of government is in a situation where the executive branch has called the legislative branch's hand . . .

And just in time for supper and deer hunting.

But what of the other questions raised? What *was* the urgency? The same day that first Chancery Court hearing took place the local newspaper, the *Clarion-Ledger*, reported, "Many legislators interpret Moore's move as a power play to force approval of the lottery . . . Some legislators were suspicious of the timing of Moore's move against bingo . . . [They] look at it as a heavy-handed tactic." And frankly it was hard *not* to view it that way, not with the Senate's vote on the lottery due in just five days. If bingo *was* a lottery and the lottery didn't pass, then bingo was against the law, too, and no politician in the state of Mississippi wanted to touch *that* sacred cow.

When asked why the newspaper had brought up the issue, Mike Moore said, "Don't ask me why the newspaper says something. I mean, I have no idea." When asked about the timing of the move, the apparent urgency, Mike Moore said, "Purely coincidence." When asked about Mike Moore's response to those questions, State Senator Thomas A. Gollott, a twenty-one-year veteran of the Mississippi legislature, said, "Well, maybe his momma and his poppa believe that." Professor Mary Libby Payne, a professor of constitutional law at the Mississippi College School of Law, said, "I'd rather not comment except to point out that strategy is most often determined by motivation."

So what were the various motivations here? Sue Hathorn, she readily admitted, wanted money. Robert Malone admitted as little as possible. But Mike Moore, what was in it for him? Certainly none of the readily apparent political goals Cathy Meeks had set forth, "to get votes and get elected and climb the political ladder."

That was January. The matter would eventually be decided by the state Supreme Court, but that would not be until December. In the interim, among other things, Robert Malone would be charged with two counts of racketeering and one count of contempt. Despite the indictments, Sue Hathorn would join up with him to run the largest bingo game in the region. Mike Moore would hire a media consultant. Nine-year-old Tricia Alexander would enter a system of child protective services so bankrupt—and as a result so brutal—that she would ask to "go home."

12

Every day there was something else, though today, so far, hadn't been too bad. The first day there had been the doctor, the medical exam that had taken over half a day. At first it had just been boring, waiting, then waiting some more, coloring until she was tired of coloring; then had come the exam itself, those long minutes of fear, present and remembered, combining because there she was, positioned not much differently than her daddy had positioned her, another man poking her, prying, prodding. And afterward, getting dressed again, putting on the clothes that weren't hers, that didn't fit quite right, the odds and ends they had found for her at the shelter.

The shelter.

A new little boy had come in since she had been there. He couldn't walk. There was something wrong with his feet. The girl in the bed next to hers had wet the bed.

But today, early, they had gone shopping, just she and the lady who had first come by the school. They had bought her some clothes from Wal-Mart. She had liked that, but it had made her sad, too, because always before her mother had been there to help her, to tell her what looked good. Now they were going to court. It wasn't much different than the hospital, really, sitting and waiting, then waiting some more, coloring until she was tired of coloring.

Away from downtown, across from Irby's Lighting and Knapp's Auto Upholstery, next to Dickie's Factory Outlet and a huge postmodern post office, sits the Jackson-Hinds County Youth Court. From the outside, the low one-story building seems small, almost diminutive, a miniature of a regular courthouse. While the scale is in keeping with the children it serves, that scale in no way reflects the extraordinary power of the judges who hold court there. These are the courts charged with the responsibility of protecting children, the courts that can remand a child to custody, order blood tests without probable cause or a warrant, or, in recommendation to the Chancery Court, permanently terminate parental rights. In Mississippi, as in most other states, a Youth Court judge needs only a "preponderance of evidence," not evidence "beyond a reasonable doubt."

The building itself is very low and very square, modern with a rounded-corner touch of deco. There is an American flag out front, and there are low, square hedges with prickly leaves that line the walkway to the door. Over the windows in the rear, hardly visible from the street, there is the heavy steel mesh often used to cover the windows in lockups for adults. Inside, a policeman in uniform wears a gun.

The lobby, too, is small. Children wait, both with and without their parents. Relatives wait. Lawyers, social workers, doctors, policemen, they wait, too, but mostly it is the children.

Judge Chet Henley's courtroom is directly ahead. Inside, it is paneled, as you might expect, and there are the standard fluorescent lights overhead, inset into a suspended, acoustic-tile ceiling. On the floor there is carpeting. The judge does not sit at a bench but at a long table. The folding chairs in the small gallery are low to the ground, somewhere between child- and adult-sized. Next to the judge, conspicuously placed, sits a large reel-to-reel tape recorder.

Judge Chet Henley is forty-six years old. His face is soft, a bit round, padded by the extra pounds he carries. He has a deep cleft in his chin. His fingernails are bitten down to the quicks. On this day he is not wearing judicial robes but blue jeans, a sports coat, white shirt unbuttoned at the collar, tie loose. With his hair slicked straight back, large jowly face, and large mustache he looks more like a figure out of the old West, more like a cowboy than a Youth Court judge. His voice is low, coming from deep in his throat.

First thing this Tuesday morning the court functionaries exchange greetings and engage in casual conversations; and it is not until you are there a few moments, when you hear mixed into the conversations phrases like "excessive scarring," "extraordinary trauma," and "threshold of pain," that you realize these proceedings are not going to be quite what you may have expected. Tuesday is "abuse day" in Judge Henley's court. Abuse day. Say it often enough and it begins to sound like Flag Day or Veterans Day, not much out of the ordinary. Abuse day.

Speaking the night before to a small group of interested citizens, Judge Henley said that in 1979, in the whole first year he was in Youth Court, there was only one case of child sexual abuse presented. Nine years later, in 1988, there were 344 cases presented—out of those, in only three cases were the perpetrators prosecuted criminally. Today, abuse day, on just this one day there will be thirty neglect and abuse cases, five trials for delinquency, nine detention hearings, three shelter hearings. This year, there will be nearly 1,300 cases of neglect and abuse brought through the court. Things are moving much faster, he says, than the system can possibly accommodate.

"You take a child out and abuse him," he adds, "and you can be sure he is going to deal out what he got. You deal them a hard time, and eventually they're going to deal it back."

Reduced to courtroom words, even the most heinous acts,

the most unforgivable crimes, become somehow abstract and unreal. It takes an effort to comprehend exactly what the words are conveying. The first three cases are, a three-year-old boy with a three-inch-long skull fracture, a nine-year-old girl who is pregnant, a six-month-old infant who tested positive for venereal disease—gonorrhea.

As the determinations for each case begin, Judge Henley turns on the reel-to-reel tape recorder. The large reels turn very slowly. Between cases, he switches off the tape recorder, and that is like a brief recess for the court, a time when it is okay to laugh and banter and talk about the weather. Joking about a young boy who has just left the courtroom, a boy who had an up-to-the-minute hairstyle, asymmetrical and two-toned, Judge Henley says that the real criminal there is the boy's barber. Speaking about a family, every member of which had an unusual, hard-to-pronounce name of African origin, he quips, "Whatever happened to Tom and Jane and Fred?" His subordinates in the court pick up on the signal, watching the tape recorder or listening for the sound of the switch. The children and their representatives file into the court one after another, about one case every five minutes, in and out, in and out . . .

What she was learning was that it was all true, the threats her father had made, that if she told she would be the one who was punished. Maybe some people would believe her, he had said, but most of them wouldn't. Her mother would be very angry. She wouldn't have a home. Everyone would treat her like a freak.

In the courtroom, when she entered everyone was laughing, though they stopped when they saw her come in, stopped and looked or stopped and started shuffling papers . . .

In Mississippi, as in virtually every state in the United States, in matters concerning children it is required by a Youth Court Act or similar law or by the policies of the various Departments of Human Services that the cases be kept confidential. The files are sealed. Access to them is strictly limited. The stated intent of these laws and these policies is to protect the children, but the result is that the systems used and the decisions made are kept hidden, shielded from scrutiny and public accountability. Whether or not the children are actually helped by these laws and policies is subject to much debate. But what is certain is that very few people have any idea whether the children are being treated judiciously and efficiently or are being retraumatized by their state's system, whether they have to endure repeated interviews, inadequate facilities, laughter when they enter a court of law. There simply is no way to know, either the systems or the decisions or the numbers; and what that allows is a kind of mass denial.

"We deny what is happening to children," Cathy Meeks has said, "and you will run into this denial over and over and over. There have been literally hundreds of studies made that covered literally thousands of victims, so we know the figures are not far wrong: one in four little girls and one in seven little boys will be sexually assaulted by the time they reach the age of majority. The majority of adult drug abusers and alcoholics were either sexually or physically abused as children. Ninety percent of the violent offenders in prison were abused. Almost one hundred percent of the violent sex offenders and the majority of teenage prostitutes were sexually abused as children. The outcome to society of this kind of carnage is that we are producing a whole generation that will be dependent on us for support—in psychiatric hospitals, in drug and alcohol rehabilitation programs, or in prisons. The figures reach the proportion of a holocaust."

Because the numbers are so high, three elements inevitably enter into the equation: education, or its lack; politics; and money. Sometimes there *is* justice for children, yet for each individual child concerned, most times that justice is not so much the scales balancing out as it is the luck of the draw.

13

*F*rom her own experience, Sue Hathorn already knew the numbers. What came next, she figured, was education, finding a way to inform people about the problem, because she could not imagine that if they knew, they would not help. All the rest would follow. So after she left SCAN, she founded the Mississippi Committee for the Prevention of Child Abuse, following the strict rules that govern the charter of a 501(c)3, a private, nonprofit charity. Those rules required that, among other things, she have a board of directors, so she began to actively recruit people to serve on her board. Operating as a charity, she received a small grant, rented a modest office, started a newsletter, made referrals—and, of course, began to collect aluminum cans.

In downtown Jackson, within view of the new state capitol and the Carroll Gartin Justice Building, the Barefield Complex is a rather inflated name for a small, two-story office building that is plain brick on the first floor and an unrelieved dark-glass-curtain wall on the second. A porte cochere extends from the front door of the Barefield Complex out nearly to the street. This freestanding structure shelters those getting into or out of their cars from the sun and the rain. To one side of the porte cochere, still on the building's front wall but without even an awning over the door to protect those coming or going, there is the entrance to a small, two-room office, which became the first home to the Mississippi Committee for the Prevention of Child Abuse. Sue Hathorn had chosen the office more for its location than for its amenities, an arrangement of priorities that bore fruit almost right away.

The first thing you notice about Demery Grubbs is that he is professional football linebacker big. He is well over six feet tall, broad in the chest and shoulders, with a very square jaw and aggressively jutting chin. He is the sort of man you instinctively step aside for on a narrow stretch of sidewalk—except that he is much more likely to step aside for you and to insist that you come on ahead. And you do. His voice is deep. He speaks slowly and you tend to listen, not just because of his size but because there is a certain authority in his words, a certain gravity. Demery Grubbs is not the sort of man you would like to see angry. It is not surprising at all to learn that his father was a near-legendary Mississippi state trooper, much decorated for bravery.

Born in Prentiss, Mississippi, a little town southeast of Jackson, one of four children, he played football in high school and at the University of Southern Mississippi. After graduation from college, he moved to Vicksburg and was superintendent of parks for six and a half years. In 1977, he ran for the city council and was elected. When, a year and a half later, the mayor died, he became acting mayor, and later was elected mayor himself. In all, he was mayor of Vicksburg for nine years but did not run again because, as he saw it, a politician could stay in office too long, could overstay his welcome and lose touch with the citizens—something he did not want to do. Thereafter, he moved on to the private sector and, after seventeen years in

Vicksburg, went to Jackson as the executive director of the Mississippi Municipal Association. He consults with cities, counties, and local governments, advising them about their finances. Demery Grubbs has found his niche: he is exactly the sort of man to sit down with mayors and city council members and other government officials and to tell them how to handle their money. As fate would have it, his new office was in the Barefield Complex, which was how he met Sue Hathorn, from seeing her around every day. While Demery Grubbs was working with cities, working on their various legislation, Sue Hathorn was working on him: within a year, Demery Grubbs was on the board of the Mississippi Committee. A year after that, he was the chairman.

"That's the way Sue works," Demery Grubbs says with a laugh, shaking his head as if he still can't exactly understand what had hit him. "Sue would ask me what I thought of particular pieces of legislation, how she should address them, what she should do. She relied on me for certain information, and I just became pure interested in what she was doing. I would end up going to her office in the afternoons and the mornings to talk about law and cases," which, he realized after he had known Sue a while, was something less than unusual.

What Sue Hathorn saw in Demery Grubbs was just exactly what she needed, a man knowledgeable about laws and legislation, a man with political connections himself. The fact that he was half as big as the side of a barn didn't hurt the situation either. Demery provided her with a measure of protection as well as a political legitimacy, and besides that she could talk at least twice as fast as he could. When she had first met him, Sue Hathorn had known that he was interested in what she was doing mainly because he had a ten-year-old daughter himself; but the problem, if you could call it a problem, was that she wanted him on her board of directors—and that demanded a lot more than interest. It required a considerable investment of time. Then Demery told a story about himself, and she knew right away that she should just ask him.

"Demery was in a restaurant," Sue Hathorn recalls, "and a man behind him was with a little three-year-old boy. The child had a cold and was whimpering and crying, and this man told the child to shut up, shut up and be quiet."

Sue Hathorn grins just a little, not because she thinks the story is particularly amusing but because she can so easily picture Demery Grubbs's cheeks and ears turning fire engine red.

"So Demery is sitting there with his grits and his bacon, whatever, when this man gets it into his mind to reach over and to slap that child hard, with the back of his hand." Sue Hathorn gets a peculiar glint in her eye. "Well, Demery jumped up and grabbed that man and said, 'By gosh, if you want to slap somebody, slap me!'" Sue Hathorn smiles picturing that, Demery's jutting jaw stuck right in the man's face. "'*By gosh,*'" she repeats with a chuckle. "I said, 'Why, Demery, you need to be on my board.' He said, 'I'd love to.'"

But there was another side to Demery Grubbs, too. He was a stickler for law and order. And besides that, he was Baptist. She couldn't afford to lose him, yet she wanted her advocacy center for children and had come up with only one way to get it.

What to do?

Sue Hathorn, being the person she is, could think of only one thing *to* do: after long consideration and realizing that there was no way around it, she decided to put Demery Grubbs together with Robert Malone.

"God help me," she said.

14

*I*n the Waffle House, not far from Bingo Depot, Robert Malone is in the corner booth, his portable phone standing between his cup of coffee and the stainless-steel napkin dispenser. He is leaning forward, his forearms on the table, a fork in one hand. The air is heavy with the smell of the eggs, hash browns, and bacon being fried on the open grill ten feet away.

"Do you know what it's like," he asks, his eyes steady in an unblinking stare, his voice hard, "when your personal and business accounts are frozen?"

He takes a bite of his hash browns before he answers his own question.

"I couldn't even buy groceries. I had hot checks out all over town, checks that would have been paid except that the accounts were frozen. Have you ever tried to explain something like that to the people you do business with and have as friends?"

And not only that, his equipment had been seized and almost every day he was in court for one thing or another—if he wasn't actually in court, he was spending all his time getting ready for it. Every day was long and hard, shot through with fatigue. It was the busiest time of his life. Predictably, many of his friends abandoned him.

But not Sue Hathorn, whom he hardly knew.

"After the raid," he goes on, "Sue was one of the only ones who still came around. She called and checked on me all the time, asking was everything okay. How was I doing? And I had nothing to give Sue at that point. She had her six thousand dollars, but past that I had nothing to give her. And it didn't look good at the time. But it didn't stop her from seeing about me."

Robert Malone pushes his plate off to one side, takes a swallow of his coffee, lights a cigarette with a quick flick of his lighter, a quick flash of the gold he wears on that hand.

"Sue wasn't just there to solicit money," he adds. "Before she gets finished with you she's gonna *educate* you about child abuse, tie up more crap for you to read than you can ever wade through," which at that point he needed like a hole in the head.

But as the proceedings against him moved forward, he realized what an asset she could be. If he wanted to continue the bingo games, to reopen Bingo Depot—and he did—there she was, with *her* charity that *no one* could question.

"I told Sue that she should sponsor Bingo Depot, that I'd have Metro Charities cancel the lease. I'd put the lease back in the name of my management company. She could have the hall and get all the proceeds."

Surprisingly, the meeting with Demery Grubbs had gone rather well. He hadn't said okay right off, but he hadn't said no either—and he *had* been sold on the idea of bingo. Already he had gone with Sue Hathorn to agency after agency, to meeting after meeting; together they had tried to get money from local, state, and federal sources. They had explored every kind of grant and endowment, and they were no closer to having a Children's Advocacy Center than when they had first started out.

Robert Malone takes a paper napkin from the dispenser and mashes it against his lips.

"I had my doubts, though, because I wasn't sure whether Sue would go ahead with it. Politically, it was chancy. Sue was well established. She didn't have any money, but she was running pretty well on what she had. But politically she was sound and this could pretty well upset the applecart."

He balls up the paper napkin and throws it off to one side.

"Sue realized that I could give her something no one else could. Everybody was telling her that they wanted her to get the Children's Advocacy Center built, but I don't believe that they really wanted that to happen. It puts a lot of pressure on them, once she opens up. As long as she's just a little gray-haired woman running around with a car, working and reporting but not having the resources to really jump up in anybody's stuff, she's pretty safe to the bureaucracy that kind of sits aside and really doesn't want to cure the problem. They just want to keep it continuing so that everybody has a job. I mean, they're not going to work past four-thirty over there. If there's a problem and four-thirty comes, it's tomorrow's problem, not today's problem. Sue's not that way. Sue will work a problem if it takes eighty-six hours straight. So you can imagine that if a person like Sue has the resources, the facilities, and the staff to go do things about this, she will overpower the state at some point or another. And they're supposed to be the experts. The state is supposed to be the expert on child abuse, not a little gray-haired woman driving around in a little red car."

But what about Robert Malone, a man Jim Warren had shown rather conclusively was not given to largess? What was in it for him? Well, he could still get paid as a consultant. He could still sell bingo supplies. And, of course, there would still be all that cash . . .

Earlier, he had explained it.

"See, it was a bumbling right from the beginning. Mike Moore's investigators blew it right from the start. They didn't know *how* to investigate bingo. First thing what you do is, you subpoena the suppliers. When you know the amount of paper used and what the people playing paid to get it and you subtract the payouts, you have the net. That's the way you do it. It's that fucking simple."

Of course, the picture might be clouded a little when the supplier is the same person running the game. And the money to Sue's Mississippi Committee? It would be an expense to be borne like light bulbs and legal fees, part of the price of doing business.

"My position with Sue was," Robert Malone goes on, allowing himself a slight smile, "if you fight them off at the front door, I'll stay in the back and make you some money."

It was an offer, he suspected, that she would not be able to refuse.

15

*T*hroughout her life, Sue Hathorn had relied heavily on her Baptist faith and her belief in God. She has always been active in her church, and the church in turn, she feels, has nourished her spiritually and helped her through difficult times. Yet at this crucial juncture, for the first time she did not feel she could turn to her church for guidance and support: she already knew what Baptists thought of gambling. Beyond that, however, win, lose, or draw, she respected her church as an institution and did not want to embarrass it by representing it in one capacity while clearly undermining its stated tenets in another. She decided, therefore, that, when she formed a partnership with Robert Malone to play bingo, she would resign from the board of the Christian Action Commission, a board on which she was a long-standing member. It was a decision that hurt her considerably. It was a resignation that Paul Jones accepted reluctantly.

For nine years, Paul Jones has been executive director of the Mississippi Baptist Christian Action Commission. According to Mr. Jones, in Mississippi there are 2,006 Southern Baptist churches, a claim that a tour of the state will appear to bear out:

in every town, no matter how small, there is at least one Baptist church, the high steeples and long, low buildings behind them usually scenic and readily identifiable. While Paul Jones respects Sue Hathorn and credits her with a legitimate willingness to help the children of Mississippi, still he was troubled by her decision to use bingo as a source of financial support.

"I do not see that an attempt was made," he explains, "or the step was taken to fund the center using money that comes from what we think of as a legal right. It may be legal," he adds. "I'm not sure how correct it is."

Among other things, in making her decision Sue Hathorn was addressing that point exactly in her own mind.

"The problem with gambling," Paul Jones goes on, "is it's the one aspect of licensing by the state that allows losers to be made by permission. What has to happen in any gambling operation is the bulk of the people who participate have to be legally made losers so that a few people can be made winners. This is the only part of state government, by licensing, that makes losers out of its citizens. We have a highway department to improve highways, a health department to improve health, a welfare department to improve welfare. You go right down the line. Everything is to improve the lot of the citizens. The state gaming commission, through the state tax commission, has one primary understanding: we must make losers out of the majority of the people to make winners out of some. It's the only part of state government that works against the majority of the people."

And while Sue Hathorn understood that, she could not quite reconcile the fact that while the church's official line was to condemn gambling, those same people weren't exactly going out of their way to help the children either. Already she had sent a copy of her newsletter to every church in the state, both Baptist and non-Baptist, over 5,000 of them in all, and with each one had gone a request for a donation in the form of a subscription. Thinking about it, she could not recall a single subscription taken out by a church.

Robert Malone, Thanksgiving Day 1990   PHOTO BY THE AUTHOR

Left: Sue Hathorn

PHOTO BY RON MOBLEY

Below: Police
officers in Bingo
Depot

PHOTO BY J. D. SCHWALM,
THE *CLARION-LEDGER*,
JANUARY 11, 1990.
REPRINTED WITH
PERMISSION OF THE
CLARION-LEDGER

Sue Hathorn (born Betty Sue Gaddy) as the Football Queen, Crystal Spring, Mississippi High School, 1954

Attorney General Mike Moore
PHOTO AS APPEARS IN *MISSISSIPPI 1988–1992: OFFICIAL AND STATISTICAL REGISTER*

Robert Malone and Sue Hathorn just after the start of their game
PHOTO OF UNKNOWN ORIGIN

Mike Farrell, Robert Malone's attorney
PHOTO BY DAVID CLAYBORNE

Attorney General
Mike Moore

PHOTO BY B. R. RASCHER,
THE *CLARION-LEDGER*,
JANUARY 12, 1990.
REPRINTED WITH
PERMISSION OF THE
CLARION-LEDGER

Counseling psychologist
Catherine Meeks, Ph. D.
PHOTO BY THE AUTHOR

Demery Grubbs
PHOTO BY DAVID CLAYBORNE

This spread: Super Saturday in Bingo Depot   PHOTOS BY RON MOBLEY

Robert Malone at his desk on Super Saturday, December 1, 1990

Demery Grubbs, a Baptist himself, while understanding Sue's position, had no qualms about bingo himself.

"I think if you polled most Baptists," he observes, "they would say yes, it's gambling. But on the other hand, of the group you polled, if you went to the bingo hall, you'd see most of them there playing . . . Sue was very conscious of how Baptists in the church felt and felt that in many ways that the church had been supportive of her, and she thought, why create a conflict if you don't have to? So she resigned her position. I personally don't think it would have caused a problem."

Paul Jones, while acknowledging that, bingo or no bingo, he appreciated Sue for her personal and her professional work—and fully intended to maintain their friendship, no matter what—did not quite agree.

"The whole idea of the Mississippi Committee is helping children overcome being made losers in their lives. Now, to use a mechanism that creates losers by its very process, it creates a lot of problems for me."

For Robert Malone, however, contingency planner and pragmatist, this whole notion was a considered part of the package he bought into, another plus for going with Sue—just in case.

"I don't feel that what we do is sinful," he says. "We don't take milk out of babies' mouths. We provide a form of entertainment. It is gambling. I won't deny it's gambling. I don't think it's wrong, though. And I don't know how anyone else could say it's wrong . . . I'm obeying the Ten Commandments as I know them, as I was brought up with, and I think God has a lot of latitude in other areas . . . I may be wrong. He may just beat me to death when I get wherever I'm going. He may just whup up on me bad, but I'll answer to it then. But Sue will be there, too, because she's got to stand beside me while we're there . . ."

16

*F*rom the shelter sometimes, if the weather was good, on the weekends the staff made an effort to take the kids out, to get them some sunshine and fresh air. They loaded up a van and off they went, the driver looking around, often checking the mirrors, trying to make sure they were not being followed.

Not too far away, there was a park in a little hollow. It had swing sets and an elaborate playground made from heavy, carved timbers. There were benches and a small building with concessions and rest rooms, everything spread out among trees and open spaces with grass.

What was hardest for Tricia to know—and she did know it, the feeling as deep as her bones—was that no one understood what she was feeling. There was no one like her, there couldn't be, because if there were they would not be able to play in that park the way they did, laughing and running, tossing Frisbees and balls, mindless and thought-less, with the joy of just being alive. They could never do that, not if they knew the hurt and the sorrow. How could you laugh then, if you knew? How could you stumble and fall and get up and go on with your game? You could never stop it that long, the worrying about what was to come, the certain knowledge of the mess you had made. You could never just play, not the way they did. She was different, and her *knowledge of that made her both angry and sad. If ever she was able to put her thoughts into words, what she would say was that she was angry about what had been taken from her, sad that she knew it could never be given back. What she would say was that what she had lost was her innocence—and far, far too soon. The problems she faced were complex, joyless, adult ones. And whose problems were they, really? Not hers. Someone else's forced upon her, made hers. And because she was still a child and without adult power, she had to believe that she had done something to deserve it, something shameful and wrong. How could she behave normally, how could she have normal friends and do all the normal things when at nine years of age she already knew about sexual intercourse? When she knew about betrayal and manipulation and self-hate? What Tricia Alexander would say was, what had been taken from her was her childhood.*

17

The caseworker's investigation was ongoing. Even though her case load was mind-boggling, she had tried to interview all those who had information relative to Tricia's case, her mother and her stepfather, her grandparents, teachers, and neighbors. Fortunately for the validity of the case, the medical examination had revealed physical findings consistent with sexual abuse—though the caseworker knew those findings could be, and likely would be, called into question in court. The results of that examination and two other things, primarily, had convinced her to press on. First, she knew that while it was not uncommon for children to lie to get themselves out of trouble, she knew, too, that particularly about sexual abuse it was extremely *un*common for children Tricia's age to lie in a way that got them *into* trouble. That knowledge was derived not only from her own experience but also from statistical studies made at Boston University and the Kempe Center, among many others. Second, the interview with Tricia's mother and stepfather had been classic, the stepfather denying everything, even the most innocent physical contact, ever, and the mother never denying that it had happened but saying over and over that she just couldn't *believe* it. There were other things, too, of course, the credibility of Tricia's own account, the way she could describe both the pain and, as important, the peripheral details, the time of day, the weather, the clothes she and her stepfather had been wearing, the positions. And there were other clues, too, other indicators, the drawings, the apparent absence of mind followed by shaking and tears. But even so, the caseworker knew Tricia's case was tenuous. She knew she needed professional support, and while she dreaded the thought of Tricia being dragged from place to place, interviewed again and again, she knew she had to call in the police and to find a therapist before, predictably, Tricia recanted, doing what under other circumstances would be considered understandably normal, subject to no questioning at all, trying to repress what had happened, trying to make all the trouble go away.

Reluctantly, the caseworker reached for the phone; but before she touched it, it rang. A report from the Children's Hospital at Jackson Medical Center. A four-year-old with a broken jaw and with marks on the backs of his legs that looked like they had been made by an electrical extension cord. For this one caseworker, current case number 197. Quickly, before she left for the hospital to interview this new child, this doctor, the parents, the relatives and teachers and neighbors, she photocopied the preliminary report on Tricia and sent it over to Jackson PD with a handwritten note on a stick-on yellow sheet on the front on which she had scrawled: "Urgent."

CHAPTER

18

*W*hat Mike Farrell could not understand right off was the why of it, why the Attorney General's Office was proceeding the way that it was against Robert Malone. In any legal proceeding, there were any number of ways to try to gain a desired result. That was the challenge of being a lawyer, the part of it that he liked best, the choice of what strategy to use and how best to put that strategy into effect. Inversely, the strategy chosen—if it was chosen with any care at all—revealed what result was truly desired. But initially he refused to believe the obvious, simply because he did not *want* to believe it. In his own mind, first he had to exhaust the other possibilities before he arrived at the ineluctable, the only explanation that, finally, made sense.

What Mike Moore had said was, he wanted to get the "bad guys" out of bingo. He wanted, as the legislature had intended, the proceeds from bingo games to go to legitimate charities. But the fact was, he *had* successfully done just that; he had chased the "bad guys" out. More than once. He had shut down a huge operation in Hattiesburg, another one in the northern part of the state called the Inner Man Church of the Future, whatever *that* was; even the former owner of Bingo Depot, Robert had told him, had been run out of town. So the existing laws could and did work and even the possibilities there had not been exhausted, for he had never gone after a bingo hall civilly: he had never simply sued to dissolve a charity as provided for by the Mississippi Non-Profit Corporation Act. If an operation wasn't a charity, it could be dissolved. No charity, no bingo. It was as simple as that.

So give him the benefit of the doubt. The Attorney General's Office had limited resources. The Attorney General could not continue to devote so much energy to bingo, which was, after all, for most people not really that pressing an issue. So maybe he wanted a way to get it off his back, to quit handling the cases piecemeal and to give local authorities the power to act. Then why hadn't he just issued a new opinion? Why hadn't he simply said, "I hereby revoke all previous opinions relating to bingo, and I am now of the opinion that bingo is a lottery prohibited by our state constitution and also prohibited by several criminal statutes"? That way, the local police departments could act or not act but he would have held up his end, done his duty to the office to which he had been elected. Why claim that individuals and specifically why claim that Robert Malone had violated the *constitution*? There was only one explanation that made sense, and that explanation revealed a strategy that was, to use the expression Jim Warren had used about Robert Malone's own motivation, not a very pretty one.

As Mike Farrell interpreted it, the intent of the lawsuit was to force the legislature to act. That was the only way it made sense. Mike Moore did not want to enforce the constitution so much as he wanted to prompt the legislature to pass a particular constitutional amendment. He was not after Robert Malone and the other defendants named—they just happened to be there, in the right place at the right time. Mike Moore had an ulterior motive, and when you use the courts for a purpose not contemplated by the law, as Mike Farrell understood it, that was abuse of process. That was why he did not want to believe it, because he did not want to think that his own state's Attorney General, the highest-ranking legal officer in the state, would misuse the rules and procedures of the law over which he had so much control. The why of it didn't concern him, why Mike Moore had proceeded as he had, what was in it for him, what he personally hoped to gain. What concerned him was defending his client to the best of his ability.

Well, now that he knew what the opposition was up to, he knew what to do himself. The Attorney General might have sovereign immunity—immunity from virtually any charges of legal misconduct, a privilege that became very obvious when Make Farrell did, in fact, file suit in Robert Malone's behalf against the Attorney General for abuse of process and the suit was dismissed—but he'd see if he was immune to public opinion as well. "Equal protection under the law" was a fairly fundamental tenet. Under the law, what was good for one man was supposed to be good for another. So okay. In this case, what was good for the goose should also be good for the whole flock. If Robert Malone's bingo was a lottery, then wasn't the Catholic Church's? Wasn't the Shriners' and the VFW's and the AmVets' and the International Ballet Competition's bingo a lottery as well? And how had a lottery been defined? The three essential elements named by the Attorney General were: prize, consideration, and chance. "Money or prizes are distributed by chance among persons who pay a consideration for the chance to win." Pretty broad, to say the least. Wouldn't that definition also include raffles and card games, even the stock market?

They'd see.

In the meantime what he could do was to contest each and every motion made by the Attorney General's Office and even initiate a few motions of his own. Then they'd get to work on the selective nature of the prosecution, the sudden reversal of previous opinions, the overlapping of the civil and criminal proceedings, the dismantling of Bingo Depot.

Mike Farrell had never seen anything like it, but now that he had a strategy himself, he felt certain of what actions to take.

All he had to do was to hang in there, not get worn down, and in the months to come in his quiet way he did just that, surprising everyone, even to some extent himself, as he went at them and at them relentlessly, like some kind of terrier, though not so much like the toy fox terrier he had at home as like that dog crossed perhaps with an American Staffordshire terrier, the AKC-recognized version of the American pit bull.

For his part, however, his client, Robert Malone, was not so focused. To him there was quite a bit more at stake than the rules and procedures of law. He was the one subject to the penalties, his business was the one that had been dismantled, his accounts had been frozen, and *he* wanted to know why.

19

Robert Malone is sitting at a table in Bingo Depot. It is midmorning on a weekday, and the cavernous hall is empty. The chairs are stacked on top of the tables, moved out of the way so that the floor can be cleaned. The overhead lights are off. The only illumination comes from the sunlight that shines through the large sheets of glass at the rear of the hall. It is eerily quiet. When a maintenance man comes in and begins to dust the floor using a four-foot-wide mop, although he is thirty yards away each stroke is audible, the mop's little clicking sounds carrying clearly in the echoing quiet. Somewhere in back, a refrigerator hums. Although the hall is spotlessly clean, getting even cleaner by the minute, there is the muted sense of the morning after a party, or perhaps the sense of a normally active ship at dock, engines off, all but a skeleton crew gone off on leave.

Like most men, Robert Malone has found a mode of attire that conforms to his work, and he dresses pretty much the same every day. This morning he is wearing a starched short-sleeved shirt with a button-down collar, slacks, and dressy ankle boots that zip up the inside. For the moment, he has turned off his beeper. A black plastic ashtray sits near his right hand. Always talkative, this morning Robert Malone is particularly expansive.

"See, what I'm saying is," he begins, settling in with a fresh cup of coffee, "gambling is not a game. Gambling is not a crime. Gambling is not a moral issue. Gambling is a business, a serious damn business. Serious money goes through bingo halls."

Given the numbers, it is a claim very few people are likely to dispute, particularly the state's Attorney General, about whom Robert Malone has, as you might expect, quite a few opinions.

"A lot of people are intimidated by the term 'gambling business,'" he goes on. "'Gambling business' doesn't bother me or make me feel ashamed. You could go and talk to a hundred bingo operators and they would probably deny that they were in the gambling business. But the truth's the truth. Anytime you're in a state, unlike Las Vegas, that isn't a hundred percent legal about gambling, then you're going to operate in a gray area if you're going to be in the business. It's always questionable. But you can't hide in the bushes if you expect to have any success."

No one has accused him of hiding in the bushes. What he has been charged with is a violation of the state constitution, a charge that noticeably affects his blood pressure. His cheeks flush at the mention of it. His voice takes on an edge. He takes a deep pull on his cigarette, then exhales the smoke through his nose.

"It's idiotic thinking, at the very least," he protests. "It's idiotic to say anything like that. It's not *my* job to defend a law that the state has written. I'm in a position right now, going to a lot of expense, in the hundreds of thousands of dollars, of defending a law that the lawmakers wrote in 1987."

The law he is referring to is Section 97-33-51 of the Mississippi Code. That statute provides that a bingo game is legal "when such bingo game . . . is being held by and for the benefit of any nonprofit civic, educational, wildlife conservation, or religious organization with all proceeds going to said organization."

"You assume that the laws on the books are constitutional. You have no other resource. A citizen is not entitled to an Attorney General's opinion. So even if you decided to check the law out, you can't. What it all boils down to is, it's not the citizen's job to defend a law. And I got sued by the state over their own damn law! My defense attorney said, 'You're the first client I've had whose defense is the law that says he *can* do it.' If somebody is charged, even with a murder, you don't charge him with constitutional stuff. You charge him with statutes. He didn't have to do it this way."

The "he," of course, is the state Attorney General, Mike Moore.

Robert Malone shakes his head.

"Politics," he says with disgust, and just for a moment his emotions are so nakedly displayed that he looks like a young boy, disgusted and angered by the fact that the game is not being played by the rules—it is a stark contrast to the harsh, certainly adult, directness of his tone a few moments before. If it is an act, it is a very good one, for it calls into question the years in between, his own background, which, for various reasons, is something that he wants known.

Robert Malone was born in Arkansas in August 1954. He lived there for about six months or a year. He doesn't remember that time and so doesn't consider himself from there. From Arkansas his parents brought him to Mississippi, which is the state he has always called home.

His father managed a Kent's Dollar Store, a five-and-dime type of store, then a restaurant. Robert Malone grew up mostly in Jackson. His parents divorced when he was twelve and, along with his sister, he went to live with his mother. The three of them moved around quite a bit, living in Baton Rouge, New Orleans, Texas. When he was fourteen, Robert Malone came to Jackson to live with his father. He stayed in Jackson throughout high school. The high school allowed him to take some introductory college courses. He chose marketing and police science. He finished high school in 1972.

As a boy, Robert Malone bagged groceries and delivered newspapers. He was a caddie at a country club, then he worked in his father's restaurant, cleaning dishes and busing tables. From the time he was little, he was interested in mechanical and electrical things, and he built slot cars and radios and worked with Erector Sets, so when he was offered a job running the projectors in a movie house, he took it and thereafter joined the International Alliance of Theatrical Stage Employes. The union assigned him to a road show, for which he set up the stage lighting, but he burned out on that because the hours were too long. He took a job as a salesman for Colonial Brick. After that, he was a route salesman for Hostess Cakes. He had his own truck. Eventually, he decided to leave Hostess and to take over his father's restaurant, but he had discovered that he liked selling and, as a sideline to managing the restaurant, he sold novelties. He sold Bic lighters when they first came out and he sold Rubik's Cubes and New Year's party supplies. He went to the national novelty shows and tried to anticipate the coming crazes, which was how he got hooked up with Acme Premium Supply. As well as various novelties, Acme Premium handled bingo supplies.

Robert Malone wants you to know all this so you'll understand he wasn't raised in some mob-type family. He wants you to know he is a local in Jackson, not some out-of-stater who came in to take advantage of Mississippi's poorly defined bingo law.

But along the way, after he hooked up with Acme Premium, some shadowy things began to happen in what he himself calls the "gray area." Robert Malone began to dance on the edge of the law.

Since he now had a line to a national supplier, Robert Malone began to ask at bingo halls about where they got their supplies—the salesman in him did the rest. By 1980, he had chalked up enough sales that another national supplier, Bingo King, offered to set him up as a statewide distributor—in Mississippi, bingo would not be made legal for another seven years. As the sales of bingo supplies went along smoothly, in 1983 he saw his first video poker machine, a computer game that simulated playing cards on a screen. The machines were brand-new, and because they so closely simulated real poker, no one knew whether or not they were legal. Their status was, in fact, so questionable the manufacturer wouldn't ship them: if you wanted one, you had to go up to Tennessee to get it. Nevertheless, when the American Legion offered to give him 50 percent of whatever the machine took in, Robert Malone got himself a truck and made the trip to Tennessee. The machine itself paid out only in points. If a business wanted to convert the points into cash payouts, as far as Robert Malone was concerned, that was their business. What did concern him was that on the back of every machine there was a switch that determined what percentage of the players' money the machine would keep for itself: video poker, he found out, could be enormously lucrative. Within the year, he had well over a hundred machines all over the state, in convenience stores and in truck stops, in veterans' clubs and in bars. In Jackson, he was threatened by other operators who envied him his growing success, a minor problem he solved rather creatively, a story he still tells with some satisfaction.

"What I did," he explains, "was once a week I went around and saw how much the machines had paid out and collected my money. When the threats started coming in, I went out and hired me two big fellas. Big." He holds his hand up over his head. "I took them over to the store and got them dressed right, put them in the right kind of suits, and for about a week, everywhere I went they followed along right behind me . . ."

And thereafter the threats stopped because the other operators were convinced that Robert Malone was somehow connected.

"It's a shady business," he admits. "The people in it are shady characters."

It is exactly the sort of uncertainty Robert Malone loves to create: is he, or isn't he, "somehow connected"? He will deny that he is, of course, but then again, who wouldn't? Within this already gray area there is yet another pocket of shadow: when, a while later, there was a massive statewide raid on video poker machines, Robert Malone had already sold out. Was it that clear what was about to happen, was the writing on the wall, or did he have inside information? If you ask him directly, what you'll get from Robert Malone is a self-deprecating smile of pure satisfaction.

"I don't even *know* any of those people," he'll say, "although I have heard about them over the years . . ."

Robert Malone kept on with his sales of bingo supplies, and with the profits from video poker moved on to commercial air cleaners, machines that removed cigarette smoke from the air. He started a company called Capitol Air Specialists, and when, in 1987, a friend came to him to say she wanted to start her own bingo game, he agreed to go in with her. He did, after all, know the supply end of it, and it didn't seem that much of a step to move on to running a game. With that friend, Bonnie Sanders, a beautician by trade, in September 1988 he incorporated a charity, Metro Charities, Corporate ID No. 0557114, and became the charity's assistant director. He applied for and was granted a state charter for a nonprofit corporation.

"What we wanted to do," he'll tell you, "was to have a charity that could give money to anybody that needed it, without all the bureaucratic red tape. We wanted to help the people who fell between the cracks of the more organized charities."

So Robert Malone and Bonnie Sanders became by definition,

"a voluntary and nonprofit organization, composed of persons who [had] associated themselves together for the purpose of sponsoring and encouraging charitable, civic work"—which they did. The only question, as Jim Warren, the state Attorney General's special assistant, would later point out, was, to what degree? The state's vague Section 97-33-51 said only that "all proceeds" had to go to the charity. But what was a "proceed" anyway? Was it the amount left over after the electric bills and supply bills had been paid? Did it include the profits from the sale of concessions, the hot dogs and coffee and nachos the players consumed with great gusto? And how about salaries? The director of United Way gets a salary. So does the head of the Boy Scouts. In short, there was a lot of room to maneuver— which was why Robert Malone felt so cheated when he was charged with a violation of the state *constitution.* He was prepared to argue almost anything—legal expenses were like light bulbs, a part of the cost of doing business, an anticipated expense— but what the hell *was* all *this* crap?

"Politics," he says with disgust.

Robert and Bonnie opened a small, three-hundred-seat game in Meridian. After that, when the owner of another game in Greenville as well as Bingo Depot was run off, out of state, Robert bought those two games as well—sitting there, as he himself likes to tell it, "bare-assed naked." Eight months after he reopened Bingo Depot, he gave a check to Sue Hathorn for six thousand dollars.

Five days after that, he was raided.

In the first few weeks after the raid, while Mike Farrell was beginning the legal maneuvering, Robert Malone considered one question over and over. The question was foremost in his mind—that same question Mike Farrell did not even want to consider. Why? Why had Mike Moore gone about this as he had? "Politics" did not quite explain it—in fact, that was a part of the question. Why would a man, the youngest district attorney in the state's history, the youngest Attorney General, ambitious, good-looking, a man who could be governor, U.S. senator, whatever he wanted, all of a sudden at a very crucial period risk alienating practically every political power base in the state? Why would he do that?

"Why?" Robert Malone asks, his voice hard, that dark look back in his eyes. "You tell me why. I don't know why, but it's pretty damn obvious: it's obvious that he has or will benefit some way from that. Even if you want to run for governor, you need lots of money. And if you help people with lots of money, they help you come election time. It's that fucking simple."

Or was it? Couldn't it simply have been an ill-conceived lawsuit that got out of hand?

"Let's look at it from the standpoint of the people who run riverboats and lotteries," Robert Malone goes on, explaining a point of view he certainly has the credentials to consider. "If you have that type of gambling, would you want any other kind of gambling going on? Of course not. It takes gambling money away from you. So why not go ahead and shut down bingo if you can?"

Shut down the games run by the United Catholic Charities? By the Shriners? The VFW? The Moose Lodges? The AmVets and the American Legion and the Special Olympics?

Well, not exactly.

A month after Bingo Depot was raided, the *Clarion-Ledger* reported, "A bingo hall in Attorney General Mike Moore's home county is recruiting customers shut out of bingo halls in Jackson."

"My understanding," said Clay Cooley, a lawyer and an officer in American Legion Post 243, "is that the entire Gulf Coast and everywhere in the rest of the state are still running bingo games."

Clay Cooley's understanding was correct: despite the Attorney General's lawsuit, across the state many bingo halls never closed their doors, not for a day.

In that same article in the *Clarion-Ledger*, Mike Farrell observed, "Moore shut down Metro Charities on the grounds that there was irreparable harm being done to the people of Mississippi, but apparently it's okay for that to be done down there on the coast."

To Robert Malone, it was apparent the state Attorney General had stepped into something he hadn't quite intended to. What he needed to do, he figured, was to find a way to make sure that step raised a stink that continued to linger, like something questionable stuck to his shoe.

Ever resourceful, within a week Robert Malone had a plan.

In her dealings with the law, however, Tricia Alexander was in another situation entirely: she didn't have any large sums of money stashed away for anticipated legal expenses, and what was happening to her obviously no one had planned.

*W*hat they had told Tricia was, she had an appointment downtown with a policeman, a man who was going to try to help her. The new lady was going to take her, the one who had just started work at the shelter. It was pleasant to get out anyway, to get away from the shelter for a while, away from the close, heavy air and the constant, constant noise. But it was spooky, too, the idea of talking to a policeman. If you did wrong, the policeman took you away to jail, that's what everyone knew.

They made it downtown okay, but after that they got lost, right inside the building. No one seemed to know where they should go. They kept walking around, passing solemn-faced men with guns and badges. One of them said to try the third floor, but it wasn't there, just more long corridors without any place to sit. Finally, they found it on the fourth floor, and the woman told her to wait on one of the chairs. She'd be back for her in a while. Right in front of her on the wall, not five feet away, Tricia saw the glass case filled with guns and knives and syringes like doctors used to give you a shot and a lot of other things—she didn't even know what they were—scary things you wouldn't even want to touch.

*"Every one of those things was taken away from a juvenile," the
secretary explained, smiling sweetly. "Children—just like you."*

*"Not just like me," Tricia wanted to say, but she didn't, because
the woman was busy again typing, then answering the phone.*

*So she just sat there, trying not to look at the glass case—trying
not to be seen even* looking *at it—but the wooden chair was too big
for her and the only way she could sit in it was to look straight ahead,
her arms up as high as her shoulders, her feet off the ground.*

*When the man came for her, he was wearing a gun in some kind
of a harness, with a gold badge pinned to the strap on the shoulder. He
was carrying a lot of papers. He said he was a detective. He said they
had to go somewhere else to talk. He took her hand and began to lead
her out the door, and that's when she felt the big rush of fear, because
she knew, she just knew he was taking her to jail. Her legs felt weak
and trembly.*

*Downstairs there was another office with file cabinets and a plaid
couch and a chair. She sat on the couch, clutching a little doll he had
given her. He wanted to know all about it, he said, what had happened.
Would she tell him? But if they believed her, why were they making
her tell it again?*

*"I can't remember," Tricia answered his first question. "I don't
know," she answered the second.*

*She saw him looking at her, his eyes direct and unwavering, and
the feelings all came up in her at once, the fear, the uncertainty, the
crushing sense that she was all alone.*

*"I want to go home," she said, holding the doll even more tightly.
"I want my mommy."*

Sergeant Mike Dill of the Jackson Police Department is forty-
two years old. His career with that department has spanned
nearly two decades. For sixteen years, from 1975 to 1991, he
worked Jackson PD's Youth Division. He is on the National
Advisory Board for the Office of Juvenile Justice and Delinquency Prevention. His dark hair is graying, combed neatly,
left to right. He wears darkly tinted prescription glasses. Al-

though he smiles often and jokes a lot, he has a career cop's direct gaze and skeptical expression. He wears his wristwatch face down, on the underside of his wrist. He speaks slowly, weighing each word, but without hesitation—he would, no doubt, make a very credible, unflappable witness in court. His police portable radio is turned low, squawking softly in the background.

As senior sergeant in the Youth Division, Mike Dill was in charge not only of the police's effort to keep the bad-ass gangbangers in line but also of the department's effort to help the children who are victims. Victims and victimizers. It has given him an unusual perspective, one he sees as healthy. One set of duties motivates the other: having seen what happens with kids too often when they are left unprotected, without nurturing, he knows how important it is to help the abused child. He has seen both the effects of the abuse and the abuse simultaneously—and has suffered some on-the-job abuse himself.

"Juvenile justice is a second-class citizen," he says candidly. "In ninety-nine percent of the cases, a youth is going to be handled by a juvenile unit; and the regular detectives don't view them as real detectives. The uniforms look at them as kiddie cops, guys who hand out suckers and coloring books."

This problem, it seems, starts at the top—and is pervasive.

"In the sixteen years I was there," he goes on, "we had eight commanders of the Youth Division. The way the command structure worked, when they were trying to get somebody to retire—or to get them out of the way until they could get them promoted—they put them as head of the Youth Division."

Mike Dill allows himself a slight shake of his head.

"And the same thing applies in the district attorney's office that applies to the police department. Unless they're good for headlines, child abuse cases are second-class cases. Historically, in our district attorney's office, child abuse cases have been assigned to the newest assistant DA, the bottom of the pole. The first opportunity they get, they dump it for burglaries and let whoever else is new take over. That's just the way it's gone, over the years."

But at least some of the problems, Sergeant Dill notes, are handed down to the police and the district attorney from the legislature.

"In Mississippi," he explains, "in cases involving child abuse, Human Services is the designated investigating agency. First up. Then comes law enforcement. That puts us in a unique position: child abuse is the *only* type of crime where we're not the primary, responsible entity in the case. The welfare department is. You have a law violation, a crime, and you got people doing the primary investigating that have no arrest powers, no criminal investigating experience. So evidence is lost. Statements are made to them that are admissible as testimony and are lost. What kind of message does that give? That this is the only crime not investigated by the police? You tell me."

The result of the second-class status afforded juvenile justice is reflected in the numbers. According to the Department of Human Services, in Hinds County in 1990, 1,339 cases of abuse and neglect were reported. Of those, according to the figures complied by the Jackson Police Department's Youth Division, 317 cases were worked and about half of those were presented to the DA's office as prosecutable, roughly 158 cases.

"Of those presented to the grand jury," Mike Dill notes, "based on my observations and feedback, I'd say twenty-five percent of those actually go to trial. The remainder are plea-bargained or dismissed for various and assorted reasons down the line."

Roughly, then, in Hinds County about forty cases a year go to trial.

"Out of those twenty-five percent, those actually doing time in jail is pretty good, say, seventy-five percent of those actually drew time."

Of the 1,339 cases reported in 1990, therefore, in thirty cases the perpetrators were tried and convicted and went to jail, a conviction rate at trial per report of abuse or neglect of just over 2 percent.

"But how many people know that?" Mike Dill asks as he considers the numbers.

On a good night in Bingo Depot, over 1,300 people will play, and the odds are, Robert Malone will make as many winners on a single Super Saturday as will juvenile justice in Hinds County in the course of a calendar year.

"The system," Sergeant Dill concludes after all those years of service, "is all fucked up."

*M*ike Farrell had already noted that the Attorney General's definition of a lottery was pretty broad, an opinion from counsel that got Robert Malone thinking.

"Money or prizes are distributed by chance among persons who pay a consideration for the chance to win."

Well, he was no lawyer, but that sounded a whole lot like a raffle to him. And it just so happened that Mississippi's Commissioner of Agriculture and Commerce, Jim Buck Ross, was running a raffle to benefit the Mississippi Agriculture and Forestry Museum. It was all part of the Second Annual Turkey Call and Owl Hooting Contest. So, Robert Malone considered, why not load up a bus or two with die-hard bingo players, bring a few *real* hooters along, notify the press, and head on down there and help out the museum? Buy a few tickets? Maybe even one or two for Mike Moore and Jim Warren?

Robert Malone chuckled even as he considered it. Mike Moore would have a fit. But even though he was looking for some humor in an otherwise pretty bleak situation, he knew the point he wanted to make was a good one: if *he* was doing irreparable harm to the state by running a bingo-lottery, then why wasn't the state doing irreparable harm to itself by running a raffle-lottery? Hell, according to the Attorney General, a lottery was a lottery, regardless.

Robert Malone had to chuckle again.

The answer to that had nothing to do with the law: the answer to that was that he, Robert Malone, was a vastly different creature from Jim Buck Ross.

Since the Department of Agriculture and Commerce had been created in 1906, there had been only five commissioners. Jim Buck Ross was the current one, and he had been in office for twenty-two years—since Mike Moore was sixteen years old. Among other things, what Jim Buck Ross regulated in this big-time farming state was, weights and measures, fruits and vegetables, feed, seed, fertilizer and soil, meat inspection, grain inspection, pulpwood, pesticides, dairy farms and milk plants, frozen desserts, eggs, honey, and catfish. He also had his own newspaper, the *Mississippi Market Bulletin*, administered a service that helped farmers negotiate loans, personally oversaw the Mississippi State Fair, and was president of the National Association of State Departments of Agriculture. And if that wasn't quite enough, Jim Buck Ross, himself a lawyer, a former mayor and state senator, *he* had *founded* the Mississippi Agriculture and Forestry Museum! What Robert Malone wanted to see was Mike Moore *try* to stop Jim Buck Ross's raffle for his museum—what he'd see first was Mike Moore being handed his political head.

It was perfect. He could have some fun and make his point, too. Hell, with any luck at all, Mike Moore might even *win*. Just the same, maybe he ought to run the idea past Mike Farrell first, just to be sure.

Mike Farrell could hardly believe it, the conservative lawyer in him instinctively wanting to shy away from the attention.

But the more he thought about it, the more he had to ask himself: why not? Why not show the Attorney General's hypocrisy? His selective enforcement of the law? Mike Moore had certainly had enough press conferences. Maybe Robert Malone was due one of his own. Under the law, there was not a nickel's worth of difference between what Robert Malone and Jim Buck Ross were doing. Mike Moore kept saying that the state was being hypocritical in its approach to gambling. Well, they could certainly see who the hypocrite was, see whether or not he wanted to afford Robert Malone and Jim Buck Ross equal protection under the law, equal treatment.

Mike Farrell looked up and grinned. In a way, it was an absolutely brilliant idea.

"An Owl Hooting Contest?" he asked.

"You bet," Robert Malone replied, allowing himself a slight smile, in his mind already hearing the rumble of the buses' diesel engines, the excited chatter of the bingo players he would take with him to the raffle; already framing out the letter he would send Mike Moore along with his chance to win.

Robert Malone did just as he had said he would—got the buses and the players and went on down to the museum—but even after he had the raffle ticket for Mike Moore in his hand, after he had the letter to go along with it typed up on Metro Charities letterhead, still he had some hesitation about sending them. Here he was, already in a lawsuit that was costing him plenty, and he knew Mike Moore wasn't going to be exactly pleased by *this* maneuver.

What the hell, he thought. At this point, I could use a good laugh.

And he sent them.

February 2, 1990

HAND-DELIVER

The Honorable Mike Moore
Attorney General
State of Mississippi
Carroll Graf Justice Building
Jackson, Mississippi 39201

Regarding: Second Annual Turkey Call and
          Owl Hooting Contest

Dear Mr. Moore:

It is my pleasure to enclose two tickets for you and your assistant, Jim Warren, for a chance to win a customized shotgun at the Mississippi Agriculture and Forestry Museum's Second Annual Turkey Call and Owl Hooting Contest.

While this appears to be a state-sponsored lottery, I still thought that you would want to support the Turkey Call and Owl Hooting Contest.

Please note that you do not have to be present to win. Good luck!

Sincerely yours,

Robert Malone

Attached was ticket No. 0081, purchased for one dollar, which gave Mike Moore a chance to win a thousand-dollar shotgun from Custom Guns & Hunting.

As Robert Malone had predicted, the news media came out in force, and the response generally was very positive.

"I thought [Mike Moore] might want a chance on winning a shotgun," Robert Malone was quoted as saying. "I bought

---

$1.00 DONATION   № . .0081

$1,000.00 CUSTOMIZED SHOTGUN
FROM
Custom Guns & Hunting, Hammond, LA
2nd Annual Turkey Call & Owl Hooting Contest
MS AGRICULTURE & FORESTRY MUSEUM
JACKSON, MISSISSIPPI
MARCH 10, 1990
Winner need not be present at drawing

---

one myself. I believe it's okay to raise funds using bingo and raffles."

The next day, the *Meridian Star* ran an editorial under the headline "Malone Makes Very Good Point on Lottery Issue," which read in part, "Mr. Moore, as attorney general, should enforce the constitutional prohibition—against bingo and against raffles, even if the latter is being conducted, also, by state government itself."

In the *Clarion-Ledger*, Jim Warren conceded the point, if not the match: "Whoever bought those raffle tickets was obviously participating in an illegal lottery," he said. "But," the Attorney General's special assistant added, "I'm not the raffle lawyer. I'm the bingo lawyer."

So what about Jim Buck Ross and the Agriculture and Forestry Museum? Did that mean that they would be enjoined as a part of the Attorney General's lawsuit as well? Hadn't the special assistant just stated publicly that the raffle was an illegal lottery, too? As illegal, therefore, as bingo?

"Warren said Moore has not received any complaints about

raffles," the *Clarion-Ledger* went on, "and has no plans to go gunning for Ross."

On a local TV station, Mike Moore himself said that he wasn't going to "mess" with Jim Buck Ross.

"Well, how about that?" Robert Malone asked himself.

For him it seemed a battle won, a point well taken and well made. Still, he wasn't exactly sure that the move had been in his own long-term best interest. He had the feeling that, if he had been some sort of Catholic, he might just as well have pissed off the pope.

Sue Hathorn watched all these proceedings with interest. She laughed at the humor in it, tried to be there for Robert Malone when the pressure got to him, even offered a suggestion or two of her own. From her experiences with children, she already knew how the legal system could be used and abused, how the prosecutions could be selective, the judges' decisions unequal and unpredictable, made between jokes and concerns about dinner and deer hunting—in fact, among dozens of others, she knew all about Tricia Alexander and the problems she was having.

Tricia Alexander was far from alone.

What this knowledge did for Sue Hathorn was to make her more determined than ever to have her Children's Advocacy Center, the way that she saw for her to strike back at the problem in all its complexity, to put together the teams of professionals that were needed, to provide a single safe haven for a child. If Robert Malone could make her the money, she knew that she *could* make a difference. And whether or not she could trust him, she had convinced herself, wasn't really that much a part of the picture. She knew herself and she knew Robert Malone and she had no doubt that she could *control* him, pull in his reins. So as the lawsuit went forward, Sue Hathorn "kept on keeping on," making her referrals and doing her counseling, publishing her newsletter, collecting aluminum cans, neither surprised nor put off when, in addition to the lawsuit, Robert Malone was indicted by grand juries in two separate counties for criminal activities relative to his bingo operations, to wit: running racketeer-influenced corrupt organizations.

The dreaded "R" charge.

RICO.

Robert Malone was now facing criminal charges that could put him in prison for up to forty-five years.

Sue Hathorn had a tiger by the tail, and she knew it; but there was nothing wrong with her grip and, as far as she was concerned, it was time for Robert Malone to make a definite commitment.

She didn't even say, "God help me."

What she did was, she sat down and figured out exactly how much money she needed, how much it would cost Robert Malone if she provided him the unquestionably legitimate charity *he* needed.

22

*I*n the daylight, from the vast parking lot of the Jackson Square Shopping Center, Bingo Depot looked quite a bit different to Sue Hathorn. It seemed more innocuous somehow, less threatening and certainly a whole lot less lively. Around the Depot, in the nearby buildings, were the U.S. Army Reserve Center, the Word of Life Church, a post office, an Eckerd Drugs, a Radio Shack, a beauty salon, the First Precinct Police Station, a driver's license office, Tri-State Semi-Driver Training, Inc., and, ironically enough, right next door with a big sign on the façade, Moore Career College, a trade school. While there were a few cars parked in the lot with her—particularly near the career college—if she hadn't seen it herself she would never have believed that that whole parking lot could be filled with bingo players' cars, not a single parking space available within three hundred yards of the door.

Nearby, she saw Robert Malone's truck parked right in front of the entrance. He had parked along the yellow-painted curb that indicated a "No Parking" zone.

She shook her head.

She herself had parked in one of the legal spots out in the

lot. Well, there was no doubt that the man had more on his mind than a parking ticket.

She picked up her big purse and got out of her car before she had too much time to think, to make herself scared. After all the feinting and the parrying, after all the subtle suggestions and all the niceties and the dancing around the edges, this was it. Today she and Robert Malone would get down to numbers. In her purse she had the legal pad on which she had figured out exactly how much she needed to get a Children's Advocacy Center up and running. It was a lot, a dream sheet, and she knew it was a risk just to ask for it. What if he saw it and said, "No, out of the question, no way"? Or worse still, what if he said, "Okay"? As she walked up to the door, Sue Hathorn had the sense that she was at one of those intersections in life you looked back at and realized what a big decision you had made, because everything after that had changed. Your whole life had changed, like when you had chosen a certain job over another or when you had decided to get married.

She pulled open the door and went in, unprepared for what she saw, the contrast to what she had seen before, the stark, undeniable evidence of the power of the law.

"What a mess," she said to herself.

Bingo Depot had been stripped floor to ceiling, wall to wall, just as Chief Bartlett had said that it would be. The bingo equipment—the video monitors, the electronic number board, the clear plastic box with the blower underneath from which the numbered balls were pulled—had all been taken. The tables, the chairs, the smoke eaters, the water fountain, the desks in the office, the trash cans, the soft-drink dispensers and the coffee urns, the refrigerators and even the frozen food inside them, all that had been taken, too. What remained was the bare shell of the building, without either electricity or running water. A leak in the roof had allowed the heavy rains from a few days previous to make a huge puddle on the floor, the same floor that before had been so spotlessly clean, shined up bright as a mirror. The air was stale and heavy, dead, without any circulation whatsoever, and had the pungent smell of incipient mildew. Coming in from the bright sunlight, Sue Hathorn had the uncomfortable feeling that she had entered a cave.

"Come on back this way," Robert Malone said, greeting her cordially.

For all the pressure he was under, Robert Malone was calm and collected.

That's good, she thought. He's good under pressure.

He led her to the back, to his office, which had an old, wobbly table and two beat-up folding chairs, furniture so ragged that the police hadn't bothered to take it; the office was even darker than the bingo hall. He sat down at the table, rested his forearms on it, interlaced his fingers. After a while, he lit a cigarette. The air was so *close*.

Sue Hathorn pulled out her legal pad and began to ask questions, scribbling the answers he gave. How much was the light bill? How much was the lease on the building? How many people came in to play? What did they pay? What about insurance? The runners' aprons and uniforms? The bingo supplies? For someone who had never run a business, she did pretty well, and finally, she got around to asking the big one: how much could she raise for the Children's Advocacy Center, bottom line? How much could she get?

"I figure I'll need at least twelve thousand dollars a month," she said. "Probably closer to fifteen."

"You can get it," Robert Malone replied confidently. "That's not a problem."

She didn't believe it.

He offered to show her his books, and they went over and over them. What Robert Malone appeared to be offering her was multiples of any previous money she had been able to raise, without any hassles or paperwork. What concerned her immediately was that she would have to be a very quick study, to learn the bingo business inside and out, so that she would know what was being done in her name. And it wasn't the world's simplest operation, not with money coming and going in twenty different directions at once—there weren't any manuals either, no way to read up on it. What she had here was the shell of a building with a big puddle on the floor, an indicted bingo bandito, and account books she hardly knew how to read. That was one side of it, but, of course, there was the other: what about the children?

But what if he decided to take advantage of the situation, to continue to do whatever it was that had gotten him indicted? No way she could keep up with it from the jump. And she would be guilty, too, if they ran a game together, wouldn't she?

Sue Hathorn closed her eyes for a moment, realizing that she was looking for a reassurance that no one could give her. She took off her glasses and allowed them to dangle from the cord around her neck, resorting to the trick she had taught herself while working in Youth Court, thinking of one child, then another, seeing the faces.

Through the smoke from his cigarette, Robert Malone looked at her speculatively, his eyes hard as glass.

Sue Hathorn started to smile, then she started to laugh. She put down her pen on her pad.

"Bingo!" she said, her decision made, thinking now only of all that money.

"Bingo," Robert Malone repeated, though his tone was quite a bit different.

CHAPTER

23

*R*obert Malone had his doubts.

He had his doubts about Sue Hathorn, and he sure as hell had his doubts about the state's legal system. While Sue and he had tentatively struck a deal for her to take over the Depot— she would, as director of the Mississippi Committee for the Prevention of Child Abuse, actually be responsible for the game; he would stay on as managing consultant—he wasn't at all sure that she would go through with it. And he could understand that. While she didn't have much money, still she was running the committee pretty well on what she did have, and politically she was sound, beyond reproach. To take over the Depot could pretty well upset her cart, particularly if he was convicted.

RICO, he thought, allowing the sound of it to echo back and forth in his head, *REE-KO*—having only begun to realize the full Orwellian horror of the charge.

First they seize your business and your bank accounts, *then* they decide whether or not you're guilty. Well, how the hell are you supposed to defend yourself when you haven't got any money? How are you supposed to pay your lawyers? For that matter, how are you supposed to eat? And the penalties, shit.

The penalty for gambling was inconsequential, a slap on the wrist and a little fine; but once you were charged with RICO, with gambling in an "ongoing criminal enterprise," you could get twenty years on each count.

Twenty years.

And he sure had been gambling, no doubt about that, running three bingo halls at once. Bingo *was* gambling, he had never tried to deny it.

But what about that state's statutory exemption? What about that? In his own way, he counted on the law just like any citizen, maybe more: you conform to the law, and you don't have any problem. But there he was, sued for violating the constitution, *then* charged with RICO, and he knew the crux of the whole thing was one state official trying at his expense to put pressure on other state officials to institute a lottery. So what else could he do but what he was doing? He was allowing Mike Farrell to hammer away at the Attorney General's lawsuit, to file one motion after another—a motion to join other parties as defendants, a motion to compel answers to interrogatories, a motion to join the state tax commission, to waive the four-day-notice requirement, to quash notice, a motion for summary judgment, a motion to stay—because there was no doubt in his mind that, if he could win the lawsuit, if he could end the game-playing between elected state officials, then the criminal charges would collapse. He was sure of it. And with Mike Farrell hammering as hard as he was, he felt certain a crack would appear somewhere—it had to—and he wanted to be ready when it did. Which was why he wanted the deal with Sue Hathorn.

Sue Hathorn would give him legitimacy. No one could question *her* charity. So if she ran the game, no one could much question him either—if they wanted to ask questions, they'd have to talk to her first. Hell, in Mississippi, just her appearance and demeanor were enough, that Aunt Sally routine, that "Well I'm not sure that I understand what you mean," her voice soft and accented like Scarlett O'Hara's, when underneath it all she was sharp as a tack. He'd seen that when she'd gone over his books. All he had to do was to hang in there, to hang tough. He just knew a crack would appear. He knew it.

And, finally, it did.

On April 28, 1990, Judge W. O. Dillard, in response to one of Mike Farrell's many motions, and no doubt in response to no small amount of political pressure, ruled that he would allow bingo to be played for ninety days "to give the legislature a chance to change the constitution." The legislature was scheduled to convene for a special session on June 18.

As soon as he heard the news, Robert Malone picked up the telephone.

"Hey, Sue," he asked, "you ready to play bingo?"

24

*T*ricia did not understand why she had to go back to
Youth Court, but the welfare lady had told her that she did, the same
lady who had come to her school in the first place.

School.

In less than a week, she had gone back. The people at the shelter
took her in the morning and picked her up in the afternoon. She wanted
it to be like it was before, but it wasn't. The teacher treated her
differently, as if she were sick. Tricia could see it in the way she looked
at her. She could hear it in the way her voice got softer when she spoke
to her, just to her. And the other children picked up on that right away,
that and the other things, like who was dropping her off and picking
her up and her clothes, which, though they were always clean, sometimes she had to wear two or three times in one week.

Already quiet by nature, Tricia got even quieter, retreating deep
into herself. Sometimes, when she used a pencil or a crayon, it broke
in her hand. It just seemed to snap. The teacher told her to quit bearing
down so hard, to try to keep her mind on what she was doing. Tricia
felt the eyes on her.

She saw them.

The first hearing at Youth Court had been the shelter hearing.

That was when the judge had ordered her removed from her parents' house and had placed her in the care of the state. This time was the adjudicatory hearing, when evidence was presented, the social worker's, the doctor's, the detective's reports. This time, the welfare lady had told her, she would probably have to talk to the judge.

The welfare lady came for her first thing in the morning, but on the way this time they did not stop to buy clothes. They went straight to Youth Court and on inside; and rather than sit out front in the lobby, she was taken to a room in the back. Even before they had left the shelter Tricia had needed to go to the bathroom, but one of the other children had been using it and had refused to come out. So very nearly as soon as they got to Youth Court and the room where they were to wait, she reported that she had to go. The welfare lady walked with her to show her where it was, then said to meet her back in the room— meantime, she would check to see how long it would be before they went into court.

When Tricia came out of the bathroom, she realized that she did not know, exactly, which way to go to get back to the room in which she was supposed to wait. She went down one corridor, then another, looking for but not finding anything familiar to guide her. After two turns she saw the lobby and, since she knew that she could find her way back from there, she went on ahead, so totally unprepared for what happened next that she froze, stock-still as a deer caught in headlights, the scene burned into her memory as deeply as strong acid burns into steel plate, a tableau: across the small lobby, in one of the low chairs, her stepfather, his dark eyes locked on her, black and malevolent, as if he had known that she would be there at exactly that moment. His dark hair was combed neatly and he had on a suit. Next to him was her mother. Her mother followed his gaze, and when she saw Tricia, her face collapsed into a whole range of discordant emotions: anguish, grief, anger, surprise, regret, enormous sadness. That is precisely the moment Tricia remembers and will remember the rest of her life. She saw her stepfather's hand on her mother's upper arm, his fingers digging into her flesh, holding her back. She saw the tears in her mother's eyes and the pure, unalloyed hatred in her stepfather's. She saw his meanness.

"You like this, don't you?" he had said, over and over, as he had poked her and prodded her and hurt her.

"No!" she had wanted to shout. *"No!"*

She saw her mother tucking her in at night, sometimes reading her a story, always kissing her on her forehead after she said good night. She felt the covers right up to her chin. She felt the fear she had known of what all too often had come next. She saw the hours her mother had sat with her when she had been sick, the sandwiches she had made for her every morning to take with her to school, the cookies inside her lunch box for a treat. Tricia heard her mother's laughter, saw the funny faces she could make, felt the warmth of her when she held her close; and she responded to all that with her own range of discordant emotions: shame and fear and self-blame and guilt and loss and helplessness so great she could not even move but just stood there, looking down, at the floor, until the welfare lady came and led her away and sat her in a chair until later when the judge would ask her to tell him all about it. Again.

CHAPTER

25

*R*obert Malone and Sue Hathorn decided that if they were going to play bingo during Judge Dillard's ninety-day stay, they had to get going with it. Of the three hundred or so bingo halls in Mississippi, Bingo Depot was the only one that had been raided. In response to the Attorney General's lawsuit, most bingo halls had never stopped operating at all, but even among those that had, none other than Bingo Depot had had their equipment or their assets seized. Robert and Sue agreed, therefore, that all the other bingo halls had a jump on them since all they had to do was to open their doors, and they set the reopening of Bingo Depot for May 3.

They gave themselves six days.

The only problem was, they didn't have any electricity or running water or phones. They didn't have any tables or chairs. They *did* still have that huge puddle of water on the floor, but they didn't have any money for advertising, equipment, supplies, or concessions. What they discovered about each other was that each of them was, for their very different reasons, both energetic and determined. Sue Hathorn had friends. Robert Malone, he had connections. By whatever name you called them, they would make use of their various and widely disparate associations, and they *would* get Bingo Depot open on schedule. Together, they made up one of the oddest business partnerships that has ever been formed.

The first big hurdle was electricity. Robert had had it turned off during the three months the Depot had been closed, and because the monthly bills were often over $5,000, Mississippi Power and Light wanted a $10,000 deposit before they would reconnect it.

"Well, Robert," Sue pointed out, "I worked for MP&L for seventeen years. I guess there must be somebody around there who still remembers me."

And there was.

Mississippi Power and Light temporarily waived the requirement for a deposit, and if Sue paid the bill on time for three months, they would waive it permanently.

"How much is the light bill?" she asked Robert again.

"You don't want to know," he replied.

With the electricity reconnected, they could begin the cleanup, and Robert began to scramble for various necessities. To have concessions, they needed two refrigerators and a freezer. Robert called the man he had bought refrigeration equipment from before. He told him what they needed and said he didn't have any money. The man agreed to take a postdated check. He did the same with the Coca-Cola Company, but that deal was a little bit trickier: the salesman agreed only to charge the company. The bill would be processed normally, but it might take ten or twelve days to arrive. In one way or another, they made similar sorts of deals for coffee machines, bingo equipment, tables and chairs—Robert had not been able to find enough tables and chairs locally, so he persuaded a man to get a truck and drive up to Arkansas to get them from the factory. The factory would bill them later. One of Robert's friends put together a cleanup crew and got to work on the building itself.

Meanwhile, Sue opened the necessary bank accounts, got the telephones reconnected, began to recruit volunteers to work the first games. Between them, they called in favors, put things on account, wrote as many "understandable" hot checks as they dared, all contingent upon the reopening and, of course, on the fervent presumption that enough players would come to let them make enough money to pay off all those bills. They didn't have any money for advertising, to let the bingo players know they were reopening, so they put up a sign in the front window; and when a reporter from a local television station came by and asked Robert if he was going to reopen, he gladly told him, "Hell, yes," and hoped he would put that out on the news.

What the reporter did instead was, he went straight to Attorney General Mike Moore and asked him what he thought of the situation.

CHAPTER

26

*I*t was the day before the date they had set for the reopening, Wednesday, May 2, and it looked like they might actually make it. The building itself was almost ready, and swarms of people were coming and going: the cleanup crew was at work, buffing and polishing and painting, repairing the damage the police had done, putting on the finishing touches; deliverymen were making deliveries, one after another; and best of all, bingo players from all over were stopping by to ask about all the excitement—many even offered to help.

Sue Hathorn was on the phone constantly, making arrangements, calling up bingo players and their friends, trying to keep up with the work of the Mississippi Committee and at the same time to take care of a hundred different details of the opening. So when she took the call from Mike Moore she did not know what to expect and did not have time to consider. But what she remembers now is that that call stopped her dead in her tracks.

The accounts of that call and the one to follow vary considerably. What Sue Hathorn recalls is that Mike Moore asked her about the conference on child abuse the MCPCA had sponsored the month before.

"Fine," she replied. "It went fine."

Then she recalls that Mike Moore asked her directly if she was fronting for Robert Malone. She remembers that specifically because it still makes her blood run ice cold.

By asking her if she was fronting for Robert Malone, Mike Moore struck to the core of her fears. He called into question her integrity and the credibility she had worked for twenty years to establish, credibility that was a prerequisite to work in her field. It made her angry because there was a presumption of complicity, not innocence—and among the many things she had worked for, she had worked for *his* election. He knew her. From her work with children and the work on his campaign, he knew her both personally and professionally, yet he had unhesitatingly questioned her, and he was not a man without power. He had a staff of investigators and lawyers and was the chief legal officer of the state. He had insulted her, and he had scared her. She recalls that what she did next was to talk to the president of her board, Demery Grubbs, and to tell him what she had been asked. She asked him to talk to Mike Moore.

Demery Grubbs recalls that Mike Moore had tried to call him, too, but he had been out of his office; so after he had spoken with Sue Hathorn he returned the call and some time later the Attorney General got back to him. Demery knew Mike Moore from his own political work around the state and was sure there was some kind of misunderstanding that could pretty easily be worked out—that is, until Mike Moore asked him why the Mississippi Committee was fronting for Robert Malone. He, too, remembers those words specifically.

"I said," Demery Grubbs recalls, the anger generated by that telephone call still in his voice, " 'What are you talking about? We're not *fronting* for anything. Now, unless this decree I've read from the court is different from the one y'all have got in the Attorney General's Office, bingo is legal for ninety days.' And I said, 'If you want to take opposition to the judge's ruling

you ought to go see the judge. We're doing everything legal.'
And he said, 'Now, Demery . . .'' And I said, 'Wait a minute,
Mr. Moore. We're out for efforts to prevent child abuse in the
state of Mississippi, and if you want to fight us and bingo
together, that's fine. Because we're going to play bingo and
make money off it and use it to prevent child abuse.' And then
he got almost apologetic and backed down and I have never
heard another word from him since.''

Which is not, all in all, even close to what Attorney General
Mike Moore recalls of those conversations.

When asked directly if he had used the words "Are you
fronting for Robert Malone?" in his conversation with Sue Hathorn, Mike Moore replied, "No. Not at all." When asked if
he recalled the conversation with Demery Grubbs, or if he
recalled asking Demery why the Mississippi Committee was
fronting for Robert Malone, he replied, "I'm not sure," then:
"No, I sure don't." On the occasion of another interview weeks
later, however, Mike Moore brings up the subject of those
phone calls himself, and elaborates.

"I think Sue is as hardworking, is as good-hearted a lady as
I've ever met in my life. I think that Sue has done some just
tremendously good work in this state to help children. I'm
proud of her. So, saying that, I worry some—and still do a
little bit—about Sue, about anyone coming in and associating
themselves with what I thought was a very good program and
still do, the Children's Advocacy Center, and doing anything
at all to taint it, to hurt that effort, whether it's hurt by percep-
tion, by reputation, or whether in some eventuality something
that Sue had anything to do with was found to be illegal. That
worried me a lot. It worried me so much that I picked up the
phone and called Sue about that—at least I remember I had at
least one conversation with her. And I sent I don't know how
many messages via people who work in the child abuse network
to tell Sue simply, 'Sue, just make sure. All I want you to do
is, just make sure through lawyers or whoever is working with
you that everything you're doing is above the law . . . please

make sure of that.' Because I felt very strongly that the association of . . . if Metro Charities was going to move in and use Sue as a front, so to speak, that that wouldn't be good."

Sue Hathorn does not remember it that way at all. Her voice is hard when she explains.

"What he said, the direct words: 'Are you fronting for Robert Malone?' . . . I would not have related that immediately to the president of my board if those were not the words. I feel comfortable in knowing that was what was said. Then I turned around and called the president of the board of directors and said, 'Will you call the Attorney General and talk with him some more about bingo because he is wondering if I am in fact a front for Robert Malone.' There would have been no reason for me to make that up."

Mike Moore goes on, "And I wonder where this information comes from, you know, I wonder where . . . because, frankly, I'm telling you—and I think you can see it in me that I'm . . . that this is a visceral issue with me, that I don't want anything bad to happen to that woman. I don't want anything bad to happen to that program and, frankly, people gonna have trouble with me, legal trouble with the Attorney General, if they try to use her, okay? I feel that strongly about it. I probably did call Demery if he was associating with her and tell him, 'Make sure, if y'all are involved in this thing, make sure that you don't get connected with something I thought was negative.'" And the Attorney General concludes by saying, "I think we've said enough about that."

But both Sue Hathorn and Demery Grubbs are willing to go on at length.

Sue Hathorn remembers that call as the point at which she began to have real empathy with Robert Malone. Heck, the Attorney General hadn't even unleashed the power of his office against her. All he had done was to give her a call. And if he had made such a presumption about her, what, in fact, was he presuming about Robert Malone? And why? Why was the Attorney General so hot after him? Or, for that matter, after her? It sure wasn't because he wanted to help her get a Children's Advocacy Center. He could say what he wanted, but he had not *done* one single thing.

"I did have a concern," Mike Moore had explained in a previous interview, on the same day he had not been able to recall the conversation with Demery Grubbs, "when I heard that Sue was about to go into the bingo business, that she not let someone take advantage of her and end up hurting all the good work that she's done—not just her, but all the people that have worked for children's advocacy groups. That was my concern, that she make sure if she is going to do that that it is a charity and that all the money goes to charity where it's supposed to and it's not put in somebody else's back pocket."

And though that does not explain the disparity in the accounts of those two conversations, it does bring to mind a startling similarity of phraseology, for Robert Malone himself had already raised the question of "back pockets." On the day that he had first made *his* observation, Robert Malone had gone on, "I hate to say stuff like this 'cause it's certainly hard to prove, but I know somebody is lining his pockets somewhere. They got to be. Why would a man stick his neck out so far? A thinking man would never have done this uncoincidentally."

But Demery Grubbs, ever the evenhanded statesman, has a far less ominous view.

"I have talked with folks that said the only cases Mike Moore tried as a district attorney were those he could win. If he couldn't win 'em, they didn't go. And they negotiated most of them out. He became so popular so fast that it overwhelmed him, I'm convinced. He came from a fifteen percent name identification in the state of Mississippi when he announced for Attorney General to about an eighty-five percent name recognition the week after he was elected . . . And I think what happened is, he just felt like he could do anything he wanted to and get away with it, politically. And being a novice in statewide politics, he let all this absorb him and he felt that because of his popularity he could do things to even strengthen his popularity more and people would follow him. The problem is, he grabbed the wrong card. He grabbed the wrong card, and this time it was a bingo card!"

Demery Grubbs laughs before he continues.

"He thinks he's invincible, his ego is so pumped up . . . The problem is, he's got a leak in his tube on a steady basis and it's going on about all the time."

Leak or no leak, however, Demery Grubbs wasn't laughing when last he spoke of Mike Moore.

"I'm absolutely certain," he says, the anger again there in his voice, "that what he said was: 'Is the Mississippi Committee fronting for Robert Malone?' That is not the kind of call you would be likely to forget. A call like that is frightening. And," he adds, "it's frightening that *he* doesn't remember."

It was frightening to Sue Hathorn as well, frightening and insulting, particularly when she stopped to consider all that she had worked for and all that she had to lose; but on that day, May 2, that fear would have to wait in line behind another. After all that risk and groundwork and with all that was at stake, right after the phone call from Mike Moore came another, this one to Robert Malone: the truck that was carrying the tables and chairs for Bingo Depot had broken down and was stuck up in Memphis.

CHAPTER

27

*F*rank Carlton is the district attorney of the Fourth Judicial District, a five-county area in the delta region of Mississippi, a position he has held for thirteen years. He is a short man in his mid-fifties, an avid outdoorsman who enjoys gardening and canoeing, with gray hair and a weathered complexion and an obvious affection for telling jokes and relating stories about hearty good times. His office is in an old brick building at the foot of the levee that holds back the Mississippi River, so when you enter or exit you are looking up at a vast, sloping, grass-covered hill that seems to go on just about forever.

Robert Malone was under indictment for racketeering in Greenville, Mississippi, which was within Frank Carlton's five-county area. Nevertheless, after Robert Malone had spent the day in Greenville with Mike Farrell and Charles Wright, his attorney for that proceeding, reviewing the case against him and beginning to prepare his defense, Frank Carlton, always amiable, invited them all out for oysters and beer.

Not far away from the Greenville district attorney's office there is a bar called the C&G that is in a converted train depot near the river. The bar has lots of old brick and heavy timbers and enough railroad paraphernalia to maintain a train-type motif. Robert Malone, a nondrinker, dutifully ordered a draft beer and sipped it. All in all, it was a fairly perverse situation, laughing and joking with the man who was in charge of trying to put you in prison for the next twenty years. Even though it was hard to see in the dim neon light, Robert Malone looked apoplectic. His face was flushed. There was a light sheen of sweat on his forehead. Once or twice he tugged at his tie.

"I learned early on," Frank Carlton said, speaking loudly enough to be heard over the noise from the after-work crowd at the bar, "that what I really liked was trial work. That's what I like. And you know what I like about being district attorney?"

He paused long enough to take a quick taste of his drink.

"Being district attorney is like having your own great big turnip patch. You go out there, look around, pluck one case or another, take it if you want or toss it back. There's always another."

Frank Carlton laughed at his own analogy, and Robert Malone laughed, too, just one of the turnips.

During the three dozen raw oysters that followed, Frank Carlton told ribald stories, mostly about himself and his experiences in the service. Then he started off in another direction, for the first and only time touching on Robert Malone's current situation.

"I got a story I can tell you about Mike Moore," Frank Carlton said with a wink. "I was at a conference that Mike Moore was going to address, and he was late getting there. One of my lawyer friends comes up to me and says while we're waiting, 'I'll bet you ten dollars that when Mike Moore gets here and comes in, he'll look to his right.' I said to my friend, 'No, I'm not going to take *your* bet.' Well, about ten minutes later, Mike Moore comes in, and he *did* look to his right. So I went up to my friend, and said, 'Man, I'm glad I didn't take your bet. How did you know he would look to his right?'"

Frank Carlton paused with the practiced storyteller's dramatic sense of timing.

"My friend said, 'Why, Frank, there's a mirror over there to the right of the door. How could Mike Moore come in here and *not* look in the mirror?'"

Frank Carlton laughed again, and started another story, for his own reasons obviously enjoying the company of Robert Malone and Mike Farrell and Charles Wright. Before he finished one last story and got up to leave, Frank Carlton invited Robert Malone to go on over to his house to have one of the hamburgers that his wife was preparing and to watch the new movie on video that he had picked up, *Godfather II*; and after what had preceded, no one was sure whether or not he was joking.

28

*T*hey did not know what they were going to do—
there wasn't much, in fact, that they *could* do. The truck had a
major mechanical problem, and it was too late in the day to get
the parts to make the necessary repairs. Memphis was three
hours away up I-55, and even if they could get there and locate
another truck big enough to carry all those tables and chairs,
they would have to take a whole work crew with them to off-
load the broken truck and to reload a new one. And besides
that, it wasn't like they didn't have anything else to do. In less
than twenty-four hours, they were expecting to start playing
bingo. Robert Malone said to let it go until the morning, to
wait and see how the driver made out with the repairs; and Sue
Hathorn had to agree. Even if they could have assembled a crew
that late in the day and even if they could find another truck,
either there in Jackson or up in Memphis, they didn't have the
money to pay for either. It was that close. It was down to the
wire.

The next morning, Robert Malone went out to borrow more
money. He had already borrowed from one friend to buy the
concessions he could not get on credit, the meat for hamburgers,

the buns and lettuce and tomatoes, the foods that could spoil. Now he needed cash for a bank, cash to make change at the door and to give to the runners who sold intermission games, cash to cover the early-bird winners' prizes. He figured that he needed about two thousand dollars to get started. Meantime, Sue Hathorn took charge of all the last-minute details, the final cleanup, the concessions, the phone calls to bring players out, to pass the word.

By noon, there was no word from the driver.

Sue Hathorn was glad to be busy, because if she stopped for a moment, she would look out the door and in her mind in every car that passed by in front she would see agents from the Attorney General's Office getting ready to make another raid—except this time, of course, *she* would be there, the director of the Mississippi Committee for the Prevention of Child Abuse.

By three o'clock, Robert Malone had enough cash for a bank, but the truck still had not arrived.

Bingo Depot was now immaculately clean and well lit. The coffee was made, the grills were hot. The chips were in racks, the numbered balls were bouncing, the PA system and the video monitors were on and working. Behind the front counter, the packs of bingo paper were in place, neatly stacked. The change drawers were open.

At four o'clock, a few early-bird players began to arrive, but what they found when they went inside was more than a little disconcerting: there wasn't a table or a chair to be found in the whole huge, empty space. The place was bare. The players stood in anxious little groups, wondering what was going to happen—clean as it was, they sure couldn't sit on the floor to play bingo.

Robert Malone began to laugh and make jokes.

Sue Hathorn wasn't quite as convinced that it was so funny.

A line formed up at the counter, and just then, blocking the view out the door completely, the truck pulled up in front and the driver hopped out.

"Well, no shit," Robert Malone remarked fairly loudly.

"My sentiments exactly," Sue Hathorn said under her breath.

Before the driver could even begin an explanation or an apology, both Robert and Sue were in gear. Every employee in the place was rounded up and put to work. One crew began to off-load the factory-packaged tables and chairs. Another began to rip open the heavy cardboard cartons.

"Buy a pack," Robert ordered the players. "Take a table and chair."

And they did, with amazing good humor. The players were not unaware of the raid that had taken place on Bingo Depot—the news had all been in the papers—and they recognized the legal threat the Attorney General's lawsuit posed to their game. Now they seemed to *like* feeling involved, rebuilding, in a small way standing up to the threat. Before long, there were work crews of *players*, laughing and joking themselves, carrying on as they carried in the tables and chairs.

A long line formed at the front door. People got on the pay phones to call their friends, other players. Everyone, it seemed, wanted to share in the excitement.

Sue Hathorn just could not believe it.

Within an hour, the tables and chairs were in place, and the people just kept on coming.

Pat Brooks, the woman who actually ran the games, got on the PA and said, "Whew!" Dramatically, she wiped her brow. "Well, now that that's out of the way, who wants to play bingo?"

Four hours later, Sue Hathorn still could not believe it. The driver had delivered one hundred tables and six hundred chairs, and every single seat was taken. There was a line at the concession stand, and the concession carts were rolling the aisles, stopping every few feet to sell a package of peanuts or chips or a cold drink. The runners were literally running to hands raised and waving, selling intermission games and making change.

Except when the big-money games had begun, for hours there had been a constant hum in the bingo hall, an undercurrent of excitement and conversation; when those big-money games had started, it had been so quiet it had been possible to hear the numbered plastic balls bouncing in the air-driven tumbler.

Sue wandered the hall in something of a daze, not understanding what was happening one dot but trying to take it all in. In the office in back, from the tension and all the activity, she got the sense of being in the command center of a big military-type ship or in a very busy air-control tower. At one table two people were counting money nonstop. Robert was behind his desk, tallying up the counts, money in stacks in front of him. The runners came in one after another and sometimes they came in two or three at a time, dumping piles of bills from their aprons and wanting more games to sell and more change. One time Robert had taken a break to go out front. He had walked up and down the aisles between the tables, nodding and waving, giving encouragement all around, almost strutting— he seemed to be enjoying himself immensely and he knew many of the players by name. Intermittently, the rustling of paper signaled the end of a game as the players threw away their old sheets and replaced them with new ones. Behind the concession counter in the corner, ten hamburgers were cooking at once.

Robert had told her not to be surprised by all this. He had tried to warn her. But no matter how prepared she had thought she was, being told about it and experiencing it were two quite different things. He had shown her statistics from a government publication, *Survey of American Gambling Attitudes and Behavior*, by the Commission on the Review of a National Policy Toward Gambling, and from the Public Gaming Research Institute, the Gaming and Wagering Business, the Nevada State Gaming Control Board, the National Association of Fund Raising Ticket Manufacturers. She had read them all, too, listened respectfully as he had explained them, though she had found it hard to believe that more people played bingo than went to major league baseball or college football or went out bowling.

"There are about three hundred bingo halls just in Mississippi," he had explained, "give or take. And there isn't a season—bingo is played year-round. Now *you* multiply it out."

Not only had she *not* multiplied the numbers, the number of halls by the number of players in each and the number of days that they played, but she hadn't even thought much about it, not until now. Now she tried to remember what else was in the statistics he had shown her.

She remembered that slightly over half of the players were usually female, and that the age distribution was, as a rule, pretty evenly spread. About a third of the players were married, but about a quarter had never married at all; the rest were either divorced or widowed. Nine out of ten were high school graduates, and almost half had at least some college. Forty-eight percent had an annual income between $18,000 and $26,000. Another 39 percent had an income over $26,000, while 13 percent earned less than $18,000 a year. She remembered that in Florida there was a bingo game that gave away a million dollars in prizes in *one night*.

Sue Hathorn began to feel some excitement herself, though her excitement was not about the game itself but about what it produced, the reason, really, that the game was played at all. She began to realize that what this was all about was money—once she saw it, she wondered why it had taken her so long to catch on. The players certainly knew it. They did, after all, spend their money on a chance to win more. Robert Malone, he certainly knew it. He had tried to tell her, over and over. And once she came to that realization herself, really *felt* it, she began to see Bingo Depot as some great, living organism. Robert Malone was the brain, calculating away. The game was the heart. But money was the pulse that flowed through it. It was everywhere. Money was literally waving in the air, waiting for plucking. Money was passed over counters, for food, for packs, for the special games and the intermission games. Money was returned to winners. Money was dug out of wallets and pockets and purses. It was spent, counted, stacked, banded, put in big pasteboard boxes. It was made into change. It was pulled out, put away, won, lost, parlayed. Money was the lifeblood of the place, the flow of it the drumming energy, and, God help her, what she could do with the proceeds!

Sue Hathorn still appeared to be in a daze, but her jaw took on a different sort of set.

That first evening, she began actually to believe that there *would* be a Children's Advocacy Center. She could see it as clearly as she could see the money changing hands. She could see the safe haven she could build for the children and the teams of professionals put together, the effect they could have, one child at a time. Beyond that she could see a legal center for children, to protect their rights, to give them a voice, and even a dormitory, a place to keep them safe temporarily, and some sort of placement type of service staffed by professionals whose manageable case loads would allow them to work with each and every child. She could see the classes that could be held to assist the survivors of child abuse and to inform the public about the problems. She could see the lectures by people prominent in the field and the conferences keynoted by nationally known authorities to keep even the professionals current. She could see a computer system that referenced the legal precedents and decisions and tracked at least some of the perpetrators. She could see so much all at once that it was very nearly overwhelming, but that first game that first night was at least a start and it beat the heck out of collecting aluminum cans. Sue Hathorn knew enough to take it one step at a time.

By the end of the evening, she was exhausted, emotionally and physically, ready to go home to get some rest. First thing the next morning, she had Mississippi Committee work.

Robert and she were the last two to leave.

"Robert," she asked, watching as he closed the front door and locked it, noting the pistol tucked into his belt, "when do we do this again?"

Robert Malone turned around and looked at her as if she were just slightly crazy.

"Why, Sue," he replied kindly, "we're back in business. We'll be back tomorrow, of course."

Sue Hathorn thought that over for a moment, knowing her mind was dulled by fatigue.

"Well, then," she said resolutely, "I guess I better get an accountant to start keeping my books."

29

In the shelter, in the bedroom for girls, Tricia Alexander was packing, putting her few possessions into brown paper bags, her clothes, her schoolwork, the few drawings she liked, the little doll the welfare lady had given her—she picked up the doll and held it, refusing to let go of it, needing the small reassurance it brought. Before, she had felt anger, fear, loneliness, despair, but now, for the first time, she gave way to sorrow. She began to cry, overwhelmed, and even though the worker at the shelter came up and held her, she could not seem to stop.

The feelings came up in her in huge waves.

Although they had tried to explain to her the need for this move, the single thing she understood for sure was, they were making her leave. They could say almost anything, but that was the message that kept repeating itself: they were making her leave. They didn't want her anymore. She had to leave. And the subsequent conclusion drawn by her nine-year-old logic was, she was bad. She was bad, and she was trouble. That was why they were sending her away.

She saw the shelter lady pick up the brown paper bags from her bed.

"It's time to go now, Tricia," she said. "We have to go."

Tricia held tightly to her doll and allowed the shelter lady to take her hand and lead her away. In her mind she saw the black look her stepfather had given her, the venomous look full of hate, and in her heart just then she knew he was right to look at her that way.

She deserved it.

She was trouble.

She was bad.

Much of the money that funds the emergency shelter for children in Hinds County comes from the state's Department of Human Services. The Department of Human Services, in turn, is greatly dependent upon Title 20 federal money for its support, which means that the DHS must adhere to strict federal guidelines. In the case of emergency shelter for children, the guidelines state unequivocally that Title 20 money will only be approved for a child's stay for a period of up to thirty days at any one place. The intent of this law is to make sure that such shelters do not become orphanages, warehouses for children. Pragmatically, it allows emergency shelters to remain just that, places to keep children during an emergency. Under the best circumstances, thirty days can be enough to address a child's legal situation and to provide him or her with long-term shelter in a group or a foster home. But it rarely works out that way. The problems inherent in this system begin to be evident when social workers' and policemen's reports are delayed, when court dockets are backlogged, when no responsible, informed adult sees the child through the complex maze of events. A child can very easily get lost. This thirty-day rule is the reason why Tricia Alexander is being moved from the emergency shelter to a temporary foster home. This is what one of the workers in the shelter has tried to explain to her, but she has not understood: she is being moved only because she has been there thirty days. If this makes sense intellectually, to a child who has been re-moved from every comfort she has ever known in the past, it is, emotionally, almost impossible to decipher; and even as this first move is made, everyone involved knows it is likely that she will be moved again. And again. In the process, she will wind up so far away from her school that it will not be feasible to keep taking her there. At midterm she will start school somewhere else. Her old teacher will not forget her, but she will not keep track of her either. The social worker will do her best, but she has another one hundred ninety or so cases to consider. The police will, as is their duty, work the case, then hand it off to the district attorney. At the new school, Tricia will make a new friend, but how long she will be able to keep her is pretty much anybody's guess.

30

With money coming in from bingo, even before she could accurately predict the amounts the Mississippi Committee would receive, Sue Hathorn began looking for a suitable house to make into a Children's Advocacy Center. It had to be a house, not an office; she was insistent about that because that was what she had seen in the Huntsville, Alabama, Advocacy Center, a warm, comfortable house that helped to put children at ease. Yet for so long she had operated with so little money, getting by from month to month, from week to week, or as she put it, "from rubber band to paper clip," she was reluctant to spend more than the bare minimum, a situation the president of her board recalls with a rueful smile.

"We actually went out and looked at old HUD houses that had been repossessed that we could buy," Demery Grubbs says. "Gary Hathorn and I went over and through this one old house, and it was just a shambles. And I remember Sue was so excited about it I didn't want to tell her, 'Sue, this is not the right place.'" His smile broadens just slightly. "It's hard to tell Sue no. And I was thinking all the time, man, we got to do something to get a better house than this."

But Sue Hathorn was feeling pressured for time in two different ways: first, she knew that Judge Dillard's grace period for bingo was good only for ninety days; and second, she had already enlisted help for the renovation. That help was contingent upon her having a house by June 1, only three weeks away, and it was the support more than the help that she actually wanted.

"It was the Junior League," Sue Hathorn recalls. "I had to have the support of the Junior League. They gave me protection, community-wise . . . See, money won't buy everything. I had to have the participation, the validation they could give me."

Politically, it was near-flawless reasoning. The Junior League charter reads, "The Junior League is an organization of women committed to promoting volunteerism and to improving the community through the effective action and leadership of trained volunteers. Its purpose is exclusively educational and charitable."

"The Junior League is made up of women who have the time to devote to volunteer activities," Margaret McLarty observes. Mrs. McLarty was the chairman of the project they called the Child Advocacy Center Fix-up. The Junior League, she notes, "is an old, national organization.""Money is raised through fund-raising events. Our Junior League has a cookbook, and we have a Christmas fair called Mistletoe Marketplace."

And it is a good bet that, at the Junior League's Mistletoe Marketplace, there will be more than a few Mercedeses and BMWs; more than a few women wearing white gloves with their calf-length dresses and men wearing suspenders with their conservative suits. There will be pictures on the *Clarion-Ledger*'s society pages. And to top that off, their purpose was exclusively educational and *charitable*.

Sue Hathorn needed a house, and she needed it fast.

"Actually," Margaret McLarty goes on, "we were involved and committed to the center prior to their receiving funds from bingo. I was aware of it and said to several people, 'By the way,

Robert Malone at his desk in Bingo Depot

PHOTO BY RON MOBLEY

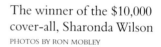

The winner of the $10,000 cover-all, Sharonda Wilson

PHOTOS BY RON MOBLEY

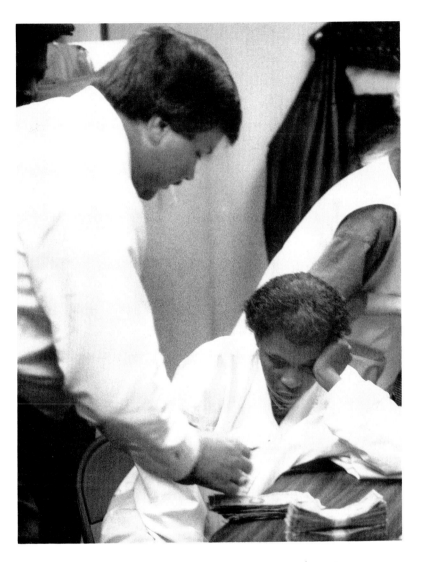

Robert Malone counts out $10,000 to Sharonda Wilson

Sue Hathorn makes change
for the players

PHOTO BY RON MOBLEY

Super Saturday in
Bingo Depot
PHOTOS BY RON MOBLEY

753 North President Street, Jackson Mississippi

The office of the Mississippi Committee for the Prevention of Child Abuse in Bingo Depot

Stephanie Bell, media
consultant to the
Attorney General

PHOTO BY B. R. RASCHER, THE
CLARION-LEDGER, JUNE 1, 1990.
REPRINTED WITH PERMISSION OF
THE *CLARION-LEDGER*

Robert Malone
gets word of the
Supreme Court's
decision, December
21, 1990. Sue
Hathorn on the left

PHOTO BY THE AUTHOR

The interview room at the Children's Advocacy Center, Jackson, Mississippi   PHOTO BY V. C. TRAU

The therapy dog for the Children's Advocacy Center, Covy-Tucker Hill's Vachss (pronounced "Vax"), Christmas 1990

PHOTO BY THE AUTHOR

Governor Kirk Fordice
and Sue Hathorn

PHOTOS BY JEFF JOHNS

they're getting some of their profits from bingo.' Everybody said, 'Oh.'"

Robert Malone considers himself a fair man, one to give credit where credit is due. And he had to give it to Sue Hathorn, she had stood right with him shoulder to shoulder when they had reopened the Depot, right with him and slugging it out, more than he had ever imagined she would, more than he could have hoped for in his best dreams, even to fielding that call from Mike Moore. Without Sue Hathorn, he was now convinced, the Attorney General would have shut him down again as soon as he had reopened his doors.

And now this.

He had to chuckle even as he considered it.

Sue wanted to get the Junior League involved with fixing up some old house. The Junior League. That was a picture. He wondered if they'd show up to work wearing their little hats and gloves and those expressions he always saw on them when they got their pictures in the paper, like they'd forgotten to drink their Metamucil the night before or were sitting on something uncomfortable. He had to give it to Sue, it was brilliant, every bit as good as sending Mike Moore and Jim Warren those raffle tickets, except *she* was serious—well, now that he thought about it, he had been, too. He wondered if anyone would ever see the irony of it, him under indictment for contempt and racketeering and running around with the Junior League on a fix-up. Not to be outdone, though, he had another idea, and he was pretty sure Sue would go for it, too.

In the meantime, though, he'd joke with Sue, "Well, I guess I better get rid of my double knits"—this from the same man who, under quite different circumstances, had bought two men the "right kind of suits" to go collect from video poker machines. "I guess I better get me some tweed pants, a bow tie, and suspenders."

Sue Hathorn had found a house, but, God help her, it was expensive—not expensive like one of those houses out by the reservoir or expensive even for a house that a family would buy and pay for over time, but expensive for the Mississippi Committee, more than they had had to operate on for the whole previous year.

Seventy-five thousand dollars.

Just to buy it.

And, no doubt about it, it needed some work.

She had been out driving around and had seen the "For Sale" sign and had called the number; and they *could* get it—the owner would opt for a quick sale—and it was perfect, old and spacious and solid, two stories, with high ceilings and a homey, pleasant sort of feel. Better yet, it was right downtown, centrally located, in the middle of things, convenient to anyone, just a couple of blocks from the new state capitol—only about four hundred yards from Mike Moore's office in the Carroll Gartin Justice Building. There was parking available across the street and bus lines ran nearby. It was perfect, but heck, they hadn't been playing bingo for more than a week. Still, they didn't have but another few weeks to meet the Junior League's deadline.

Well, she guessed she'd just have to turn up the heat on Robert Malone.

Robert Malone said, "Buy it."

There was, however, one little problem. Money. The Mississippi Committee could not borrow that much, and certainly it had nowhere near enough on hand.

"How much *do* you have?" Robert had asked her.

"Well," she had replied, "we have most of that six thousand you gave us back in January."

The best deal she had been able to work, she had explained, was to get the owner to finance them by giving them time to make three separate payments. Twenty-five, twenty-five, and twenty-five thousand dollars.

"Go ahead to the closing on the house in time to meet your deadline," Robert advised her. "Use the money you have as earnest money. I was planning to run a big game June 2 anyway. That's a Saturday. Tell them you'll have the first payment the Monday after that. That's the fourth."

Once again, Sue Hathorn could not believe it. It had been just a month and two days since their first game.

"Robert," she asked, "are you sure?"

Robert Malone gave her his most withering look, refusing to answer, then his face brightened.

"But, hey, Sue, I got this other idea."

31

*L*iz Taylor is a petite woman with straight silver hair cut short. She is dynamic, full of energy. Her voice is heavily accented yet husky. Originally from McComb, Mississippi, when she moved to Jackson she shortened Mary Elizabeth to Liz. When she got married, she changed her maiden name, Billings, to Taylor. Liz Taylor. Like the better-known Liz Taylor, this Liz Taylor from Jackson most often wears fashionable dresses and an abundance of jewelry. Most times, she is quick to laugh and to make jokes.

Liz Taylor has known Sue Hathorn for about twenty years. They met when Sue was working at Youth Court, and over the years they stayed in touch and became friends. From 1986 until 1989, Liz Taylor was volunteer coordinator for the Jackson Rape Crisis Center, and when Sue Hathorn wanted to start a CASA program in conjunction with the Mississippi Committee, Liz Taylor seemed the perfect choice. Sue asked her; Liz agreed. It was to get money to be eligible to receive matching funds from the state for the CASA program that prompted Sue Hathorn initially to approach Robert Malone.

"CASA stands for Court-Appointed Special Advocate," Liz

Taylor explains. "I recruit and train volunteers and we go into Youth Court with neglected and abused children. We are appointed by the Youth Court judge, and we work with this one child to be sure the child is being protected. We go back and make all of our reports to the judge and make recommendations at the time of the hearings, to make sure the judge has all the necessary information."

Although the local chapters that provide such advocates vary greatly, CASA is a national program now in forty-seven states. Started in 1977 by a Supreme Court judge in Seattle, Washington, the program is not without controversy: many knowledgeable people criticize it for its reliance on volunteers, a practice that can be interpreted as minimizing the state's obligation to children, and for allowing nonlawyers who may know little or nothing about the issues to become part of the system. In the absence of dedicated prosecutors, however, and without funds to assign a law guardian, a lawyer who is charged with the specific task of representing the best interests of an individual child, both Sue Hathorn and Liz Taylor believe that some help is better than none, which is why they were working together in June 1990.

Liz Taylor had been away at a conference, and it was only when she returned that Sue told her about bingo and not just about that: Sue popped the news that they were moving the office of the Mississippi Committee *into the bingo hall*. That was the idea that Robert Malone had come up with, though the same idea had occurred to Sue Hathorn at just about the same time. Robert Malone had seen the move as a way to increase his protection. Once the move was made, if anyone wanted to raid Bingo Depot, they would have to walk, quite literally, right past the office of the Mississippi Committee for the Prevention of Child Abuse. Sue Hathorn saw the move as a way both to keep a close eye on the game and to save on the rent for the office in the Barefield Complex. Liz Taylor saw it as a nightmare.

"I was shocked," she recalls. "I was floored. My first initial reaction was sheer shock . . . I mean, I could not believe what

I saw. Here we go into this huge hall, and Sue said, 'This is going to be our new office.' And I thought, my God. It was just so overwhelming, this huge bingo hall, and here we were going to work to prevent child abuse in a bingo hall. I can't even describe it. It was a nightmare.''

Liz Taylor's reaction still makes both Sue Hathorn and Robert Malone laugh.

"Liz just about died," Robert starts. "First, she had to come to South Jackson every day, then she had to have an office in a goddamn bingo hall."

"Liz never told her daughter from Houston where she worked," Sue Hathorn goes on. "Then her daughter came in, and said, 'Why, Mother, your office is in a bingo hall!' I mean, it just about killed Liz."

"I was basically there about seven months," Liz Taylor notes. Though usually she is very quick to laugh and to make jokes, about this she still finds it hard to smile. "That was the longest seven months of my entire professional career."

32

*J*ust as Robert Malone had advised her, Sue Hathorn put up her earnest money toward the house at 753 North President and went ahead to the closing. That first Super Saturday after the raid on Bingo Depot was an overwhelming success, and on Monday, just as he had said he would, Robert Malone gave Sue the twenty-five thousand dollars.

Sue Hathorn was, as might be expected, ecstatic. *This* she really could not believe.

She had a house.

She had a house for a Children's Advocacy Center.

But it took her only about sixty seconds to realize that the house alone was not nearly enough. The house had to be renovated and the rooms altered to accommodate new functions. She had to assemble a staff and she had to be sure she could pay them. She needed office supplies, office furniture, furniture for children, and special equipment. She needed to head off the inevitable turf wars that would develop when she actually opened the center—she would have to reassure the Department of Human Services, the Jackson PD, and the district attorney that she was only trying to coordinate their efforts and not taking over their jobs. She had so much to do and so little time to do it in that, briefly, she felt overwhelmed. So she did what she had done for the last thirty-one years: first thing, she talked to her husband.

After Betty Sue Gaddy's fiancé was killed just a few days before the date set for their wedding, Betty Sue decided that she did not want to love anymore. She had learned with certainty the hurt that caring could bring, and for two years she did not date at all. She wouldn't risk it. Finally, however, a woman at work begged her to go out on a double date: the woman wanted to date a young man from Hinds Junior College, but the young man's roommate did not have a date—and he would not go out without him. Betty Sue said no, she didn't date anymore, but the young woman was relentless, and she did, at last, persuade Betty Sue to go to the Firemen's Ball.

"I loved to dance," Sue recalls, "but Gary didn't. I didn't remember his name. He didn't remember my name. But we made a date for the next night, and both of us had to call to get each other's name."

Gary Hathorn had recently returned from four years in the Coast Guard. What attracted Gary to Sue was her personality.

"She just bubbles over," he says. "That's what it was. Her whole personality."

Within a short period of time—by Sue's account fifteen days; by Gary's, five weeks—he asked her to marry him, and they were engaged. A year later, they were married.

While still a student at Hinds Junior College, Gary Hathorn had gotten interested in architecture as well as in Betty Sue Gaddy. While he went on to Mississippi State and earned a degree in civil engineering, he never lost that interest, and at the first opportunity he took a job with an architect. He worked long enough and accumulated enough experience to be allowed to take the licensing exam; he passed it and became a registered architect.

"I'm lucky because I have Gary," Sue Hathorn says. "He's where I get my strength. I know he'll be there. Once or twice a year, I get so angry or so frustrated about something and I'll call him and somehow he'll know how important it is and he meets me right then. He's walked out of meetings because he knows I have to see him right then; and in fifteen minutes I can go back to it." She pauses before she adds, "Gary is all I have."

So when Sue Hathorn was feeling overwhelmed by all that she still had to do to open the advocacy center she wanted so badly, it was only natural for her to turn to Gary, and it didn't take long for him to give her the reassurance she sought—and for her to enlist the help of her very own registered architect.

When Gary Hathorn saw the house at 753 North President, his first thought was that it had a lot of potential—after the house he had inspected for Sue before, he also felt a good deal of relief. This big eighty-year-old two-story bungalow was good and solid. Sure, there were a few indications that the house had settled some over the years, but that was nothing more than he would have expected in a house built in 1910. Other than that, there were cracks in the plaster that had to be patched. The wallpaper needed replacing, and the floors could use refinishing. The major work to be done involved replacing the floor furnace and gas space heaters with central heat and air. Nothing too major. With a little cosmetic work on the inside and a bit of maintenance on the exterior, the house was usable pretty much just as it was. Fortunately, only a few small changes had been made inside, so the bedrooms could easily be converted into offices and the dining room made into the interview room that Sue said had to be at the center of everything. It was certainly possible to make the house wheelchair-accessible and to bring it all up to code. Overall, Gary had to say that he was pleasantly surprised by the house Sue had finally come up with—and he was pleasantly surprised again with the help the Junior League sent to aid in the fix-up.

Despite Robert Malone's reservations, the Junior Leaguers did not show up wearing hats and white gloves. The first person Margaret McLarty sent over was Beth Green, an interior designer with her own firm. Beth Green set to work selecting colors and materials and fabrics, and the other volunteers sandpapered and peeled the old wallpaper from the walls. Of course, the money Robert Malone and bingo provided made its own contribution, but considering the diversity of the participants, the renovation proceeded extraordinarily well. In the meantime, Sue Hathorn put together a budget for the center and prepared to move the offices of the Mississippi Committee into Bingo Depot. As much as anyone, she was aware of how soon the ninety-day stay for bingo was due to run out, and with the way Robert's luck had been running, heck, they'd probably close it up before that. Robert's legal motions had been denied one after another, and Judge Dillard, it seemed, was not prone to consider any new ones, not that that slowed down Robert's attorney, Mike Farrell, one bit. He just kept filing motions, one after another.

"It seemed like you could never win," Robert Malone recalls, "not one fucking inning."

All in all, had she had the vocabulary, that was a sentiment Tricia Alexander might well have echoed exactly.

*I*t *seemed as though she had been in the new place only a few days, hardly long enough even to get settled in, when the temporary foster-care lady told her they were going downtown. They were expecting her. Tricia did not know how to take that exactly, what that meant.*

From the suburb on the outskirts of Jackson the foster-care lady got on I-55, then turned off it at the Pearl Street exit. At the first red light, she stopped and pointed off to the left.

"That's where we're going, the Hinds County Courthouse," she said. "See? We're almost there, easy as pie."

But parking places were scarce. The parking lots were all private, reserved for government workers and lawyers, and as they circled the area looking for a place to park, Tricia recognized the headquarters of the Jackson police. They passed right by it. She looked at the door and remembered the Youth Division they had had so much trouble finding, her and the shelter lady that time; and she remembered the interview there, the big chairs, the man with a gun, the display case filled with weapons and bottles and drugs.

In front of this building, the Hinds County Courthouse, there was a war memorial that looked like a rocket. All the names on it, this lady said, were names of people who were dead. Behind it, there was the courthouse itself, with a long flight of stone steps and big brown rectangular windows. The building was tan, and the doors were so big and heavy it took the foster-care lady's both hands to open one. Inside, there were big, square columns and the floors were all made of stone. It was dark and dim and deserted. Their footsteps echoed down the big halls and up the big stairway. The place was very solemn, solemn and scary. This lady wasn't sure where to go either, and there was no one at the information desk.

After a while, they took the elevator to the third floor, then they changed elevators to go on up to the fifth floor. It was better up there. Just as you got out of the elevator, there was a skylight that let in some sun.

"Here we are," the foster-care lady explained. "This is the district attorney's office."

They sat down to wait, and a little while later a lady came out to meet them. Even before they went on back to her office, Tricia knew exactly what to expect. She could see it in the lady's face, the questions. She would want to know all about it, what had happened. She would ask her about what she had said.

"They don't believe me," Tricia said to herself. "They keep asking me over and over"—like her mother did when she knew she was lying.

"See those little windows over there?" the attorney lady asked. "Those are the windows the prisoners used to look out of. This used to be the jail."

Tricia looked at the little windows, and in her mind she began to practice the answers that had worked pretty well with the policeman.

"I don't know," she said to herself. "I can't remember."

Cathy Meeks is wearing a long black dress with a tan belt and low-heeled tan boots. She is addressing a group of CASA volunteers who have yet to be assigned their first case. Her voice is low and soothing, yet sometimes, when she comes to a point in her talk that affects her deeply, her eyes close just for a moment longer than a blink: it is a pause, almost, in her seeing, as if she is trying for that fraction of a second to shut out the horrors she has seen.

"The thing that a child fears most is abandonment," she begins, "abandonment by their trusted caretaker. Your idea of a trusted caretaker and my idea of a trusted caretaker may be slightly different than an abused child's. Even an abusive parent, if the child has bonded with that parent, to that child that parent is the key to that child's survival. Even if they beat them up, even if they starve them or sexually abuse them. The reasoning goes: Well, I've gotten this far . . . Abandonment is the thing the child fears most. Remember that motivation."

Cathy Meeks stops only long enough to look at her small audience, to see whether or not there are questions. Then she goes on.

"So here's a child who is seven or eight years old and for one reason or another—maybe Mom has just remarried and the stepfather has come into the home—a new parent has come into the home. And so she's even more attached to Mom because this is the only bonded caretaker she has. And Mom says, 'Please love him. I want him to be part of our lives. He's important. Let's be a family.' And say, then after a few weeks Mom goes out and the stepfather begins to fondle the child. But he doesn't just do it and walk away. The first thing he does, he entices her. He tells her, 'Mommy would really appreciate it if you made me happy. And you know what would make me happy? If you sat on my lap. And if you sit on my lap, maybe I'll buy you that puppy you wanted. And let me tell you, too, what we've been doing here today is our little secret. This is just between you and me. But if you tell about this, I'm going to be real unhappy and your mom will, too. And you know what? She won't believe you. She won't believe you because she loves me. And what she'll probably do is send you away. She may even send you away to jail. A policeman will come and get you.' And the child will believe that in a second. So what we've got is the fear of abandonment and the natural narcissism of the child that makes them believe they are somehow responsible for the happiness of the parent and for keeping the family together. If you can understand this little scenario you will be able to understand why most children keep their secret to their graves."

Cathy Meeks's eyes close for just an instant longer than a blink.

"All the factors operate for them to maintain the secrecy."

Linda Anderson is the assistant district attorney in charge of child abuse for Hinds County. She has been in that position for two years. Her predecessor was Tommy Green, and before that it was Cynthia Hewes. Before too long, as Sergeant Dill had predicted, Linda Anderson will move on herself, and Cynthia Hewes and Bobby DeLaughter will split her cases between them.

"Burnout is a problem," Linda Anderson admits right from the start. "It is the kind of work that is hard to leave at the office. It gets to you. Some days, I long for just a good old burglary, a shooting."

Linda Anderson went to the Mississippi College Law School—before that she was a teacher. She has two children. She has dark eyes and an oval face. Her hair is pulled back in a ponytail, and she wears hoop earrings.

In her small office, Linda Anderson explains that too many people assume that, after a police report is made, a person is automatically charged with a crime. It just doesn't work that way, she says. It is part of her job to review the police report, to evaluate the evidence, and to interview the people involved before deciding whether or not to charge someone with a crime.

But there are real problems, too, other than the burnout and that misconception that may not be so readily apparent.

In Hinds County, in the previous six months, seven assistant district attorneys waited to go to court before only four judges, two civil and two criminal. Prior to that, there had been three judges for civil proceedings and only one judge for criminal cases. And if that one judge in Criminal Court was held up in, say, a capital murder case, court dates could be delayed for two to four months. Cases were bumped back when they were not resolved or when other cases went on to trial.

When asked about the number of cases actually processed through her office, Linda Anderson starts her reply by talking about time.

After a report of child sexual abuse is made, she says, it takes about four to six weeks for the police report to reach her. If after she has reviewed that report she decides to proceed, the case may be six weeks getting to the grand jury. Then the accused has to be served with a notice of indictment. After that, there will be a preliminary hearing and only then will the circuit court administrator set a court date. Most times, she says, it takes from a year to a year and a half for her to get a case into court. She admits that no numbers are kept, the number of reports sent over from the Jackson PD compared with the number of cases accepted. Their office does not have the manpower for that, she says. And there are other problems, too, with legal precedents and decisions, with children as witnesses, with the fact that it is usually not the strongest cases that end up in court—in a very strong case the defendant is likely to plead guilty and to take his or her chances with the sentencing.

But Linda Anderson seems genuinely to care about the cases in which she is involved and she speaks proudly of the district attorney's Victim Witness Program, which takes the children through the building and the courtroom to familiarize them with the setting before they have to go in to testify. Still, she is just one person, one very busy attorney in what amounts to a temporary position, and according to the Jackson Police Department's Youth Division, in the last calendar year 158 cases, give or take, were sent over as prosecutable.

"And then you have a seven-year-old," Cathy Meeks goes on, "who, upon questioning, reveals sexual abuse. Do you believe them? Remember: everything operates for them *not* to tell. Do you believe them? I do. Because essentially what they would be doing is making up a story that gets them *into* trouble, a story that could well lead to the abandonment they fear so much. It goes against everything that operates in a child. Yes, children *do* lie about sex abuse: they lie and say that it didn't happen when it really did. I have seen over three hundred children to date, and only one time, for various reasons, did I even think that the child might have been lying."

In the Hinds County Courthouse, the courtroom is very official-looking, brown and heavy, with brown wood trim, brown furniture, a brown judge's bench. Art deco lights are hung from cables that run down from the high ceiling. They cast a yellow-brown light. Even for an adult, the space is intimidating, successfully conveying the somber power of the law. When court is in session, there is a court reporter, a judge, a jury, lawyers, and defendants; and even for an adult—much more so for a child—it is terrifying to think of being in that space in front of all those people telling your deepest, darkest, most embarrassing personal secrets.

Liz Taylor just *thought* she knew about nightmares.

34

*A*fter Sue Hathorn had made the decision to move the office of the Mississippi Committee to Bingo Depot, Gary Hathorn drew up some plans; but the plans Gary provided set out a space more elaborate than Sue had in mind. What Sue wanted was just two walls built into the existing corner near the entrance to the Depot to make a single square room—as far as she was concerned, the walls didn't even have to go all the way to the ceiling. For that she didn't really need an architect, so once it was clear what she wanted, Robert Malone got a couple of carpenters and they went to work. The carpenters built two partitions that, in fact, did not go anywhere near as high as the ceiling, and for about nine hundred dollars, including the wiring, the Mississippi Committee had a new office. They moved in in July, on the weekend of Jubilee Jam, a local celebration during which most of the streets downtown were blocked off.

Even as they moved in, it was obvious that the office was too small. Every desk top and corner was covered. There were chairs put in stacks, typewriters on the chairs, boxes of paper and files on and beneath every table. In all, in that small corner office there were six desks, five three-by-five tables, two video machines, two telephone answering machines and two copiers. On the wall behind Sue Hathorn's desk was a piece of needle-point in a frame on which was sewn, "Patience is the ability to idle your motor when you feel like stripping your gears." Behind Liz Taylor's desk was a teddy bear wrapped in hygienic plastic. In front of the desk reserved for Dana Gardner, there were two car seats for children. Sue Hathorn had had a poster made up with a logo for the Children's Advocacy Center. It was mounted, wrapped in clear plastic, and moved from place to place whenever it got in the way. The poster showed a simple, childlike drawing of a house with a smiling sun over it. On every telephone receiver, Robert Malone placed an electronic device that detected bugs on the line.

35

*F*or the next six weeks things remained in an active sort of stasis. Work on the house at 753 North President continued, Liz Taylor reported for work at the Depot, Mike Farrell continued to work over the judges. Robert Malone ran game after game, and Sue Hathorn, when she was not doing work for the Mississippi Committee, stepped out of her office and worked as a volunteer, making change and selling cards during the games. She put a bulletin board up near her door and on it displayed pictures of severely abused and missing children.

Judge Dillard's ninety-day stay was set to expire July 26, but in the meantime, both Robert and Sue were determined to forge on ahead until somebody or something stopped them. At night, they would take a break and drive around together, checking out the action at the other bingo halls, counting the cars parked in the lots, determining their share of the market. Sue learned to ask questions like "Did they make their door tonight?" and "How big was their payout?" and Robert Malone began to keep track of his answers.

On July 26, Judge Dillard refused to extend his ninety-day stay, but the state Supreme Court overruled him: in response to an appeal to stay the injunction, the Supreme Court expedited its schedule to hear the arguments pro and con about whether or not bingo was, indeed, a lottery and, in addition, the court ordered that bingo could continue to be played in the interim.

On September 20, at the request of Ed Peters, the Hinds County district attorney, Judge William Coleman of the county circuit unexpectedly dismissed Hinds County's criminal charges against Robert Malone. The order of *nolle prosequi* cited "identical issues of law and fact" in the civil and the criminal proceedings. "The same conduct," the order read, "and/or course of conduct alleged herein to be a criminal violation forms the basis of the civil action . . . the State feels that the end of justice will be served by the entry of a *nolle prosequi* herein." So Judge Coleman ordered and adjudged, and those particular criminal charges against Robert Malone were dismissed. Ed Peters did not wish to prosecute.

Attorney General Mike Moore hit the roof.

"I am appalled that this case was settled without any consultation with my office," the *Clarion-Ledger* quoted him as saying. "Metro Charities made a mockery of the law."

"Attorney General Mike Moore," Robert Malone was quoted in the same article, "has done more to destroy the structure of charity fund-raising in Mississippi than any other person."

"I wonder how much," Sue Hathorn said to no one in particular, "we can make in the next couple of months."

"The Hinds County action," Mike Moore continued, "will not affect a similar case in Washington County."

But as the statements went on and each side had its say, despite the adversarial perspectives two things were for certain: the Supreme Court would have *its* say and that certainly *would* affect all that would follow; and now without doubt the gloves would come off. Since one court had now ruled that the civil and the criminal proceedings overlapped, the Attorney General's Office would pursue its civil suit with a vengeance. Mike Farrell was aware of that and was aware, too, that all of his

motions and all of Robert's various shenanigans had undoubtedly angered the chief legal officer of the state, a man with a
whole *staff* of attorneys.

There was little doubt at all but that both sides would be
ready October 22, the date the Supreme Court had set for their
hearing.

36

The Supreme Court of the state of Mississippi is located on the ground floor of the Carroll Gartin Justice Building, two floors down from the offices of the state Attorney General. Mike Moore and his staff were able to come down to the hearing by elevator, but everyone else in attendance had to make their way through a raw, gray, blustery fall day—and many had. By 8 A.M. on that Monday, October 22, a crowd had already begun to assemble in the lobby outside the Supreme Court. Policemen in uniform maintained order in the press of lawyers from all over the state, newspaper reporters and television crews, interested spectators, representatives from various charities, and professional bingo operators.

Inside the courtroom, the nine justices' high-backed, well-cushioned swivel chairs were arranged in a semicircle, facing out. The rear wall of the courtroom was also semicircular, but it faced in. Overhead, fluorescent panels and harsh mercury-vapor lamps repeated the curving shapes, and the light cast was pale and flat, as colorless as a lawyer's most technical argument. Soon after the doors were opened, all the seats in the gallery were taken. Shortly thereafter, when the standing-room area was filled, the uniformed policemen began to turn people away at the door. A crowd remained in the lobby.

Sue Hathorn was wearing red—red blazer, red skirt, white blouse, and red shoes—making her stand out among all the charcoal-gray suits. Around her neck were half-frame reading glasses that hung from a red cord. While waiting for the arguments to begin, she read the transcript of another trial, one, predictably, that involved the case of a child. Nearby, Liz Taylor sat ready with her phone and her beeper.

Mike Farrell's mother came in and sat directly behind him, waiting to watch her son plead before the Supreme Court. Until he stood up to begin, she pressed her knuckles against her chin. As she listened, her hand fell away to her side.

Robert Malone was wearing a blue blazer, gray slacks, white shirt with purple stripes and matching purple-red tie. His ankle boots zipped up the side. He sat hunched forward, his hands clasped between his knees, his eyes fixed on whoever was speaking. His cheeks were flushed crimson. It was obvious he would have preferred to be almost anywhere else. Just for a moment before the nine justices—seven white men, one black man, one white woman—filed into the courtroom, he glanced at Sue Hathorn. In his glance there was anger, expectation, uncertainty, hope.

At 9:24, the Attorney General of the state of Mississippi, Mike Moore, arrived. Attorney General Moore was wearing a starched blue shirt with a button-down collar, darker blue tie, conservative gray suit. He shook hands all around on his side of the court, heartily greeting, for the most part, members of his staff. Before he sat down, he waved across the courtroom to Mike Farrell. Directly behind Mike Moore sat Stephanie Bell, his newly hired media consultant. Twice, Stephanie Bell leaned forward to say something, to which the Attorney General did not reply but only nodded. For this case, Mike Moore would let Jim Warren actually make the presentation. As arguments were made, Mike Moore would tuck his upper lip between his teeth and chew it, change from one earnest look to another, head cocked to one side, eyes down, then up. He would rest his elbows on the arms of the chair and interlace his fingers just below his chin, not quite in front of his face.

When the nine justices filed in and took their seats, it was readily apparent that they were all substantially older than any of the principals involved. When Mike Farrell was directed to proceed in the matter of case number 90-CA-0568, he did so in complete silence. Not a single throat was cleared. There was not a single suppressed cough or hushed aside.

Mike Farrell began his presentation by referring back.

"Any construction of our constitution," he posited, "requires an examination of the historical setting to determine the precise evil that the constitutional framers sought to prevent or remedy."

In short, he would argue, the framers of the state constitution did not *intend* to prohibit bingo when they prohibited lotteries. In order to understand the historical setting of the state's constitutional ban on lotteries, he would explain, it is necessary to look beyond Mississippi, because lotteries were a nationwide trend in the 1800s, when the state constitution was written.

"Indeed," Mike Farrell went on, "this court must look beyond our own colonial history to understand why our own constitution even mentions lotteries."

Mike Farrell then proceeded to give a fascinating history of lotteries, and although the history was interrupted by questions from the justices, the text, as quoted verbatim below, was contained in his brief.

"Lotteries date back to Roman times," he began. "Augusta Caesar is credited with sponsoring the first known public lottery, in order to raise funds to repair the city of Rome. Feudal princes of Europe continued the custom of lotteries to raise money. Lotteries were common in medieval Italy. Francis I of France established a government *loterie* in 1539. Queen Elizabeth of England chartered a lottery in 1566.

"Lotteries helped finance colonial America from the beginning. In 1612, the Virginia Company petitioned the King of

England to conduct a lottery to help finance its beleaguered Jamestown settlement. Virginia passed a state-sponsored lottery in 1754 to raise funds to build fortifications against the French. Lotteries were commonly used to build bridges, roads, schools, and colleges. King's College in New York, now Columbia University, was the first college to seek funding with a lottery. Not to be outdone, Princeton and Harvard followed suit. In 1768, George Washington sponsored a lottery to build a road . . . New York and Massachusetts were the first states to limit lotteries to those approved by the legislature. Many other states followed suit in a familiar pattern: a group of citizens would petition the legislature or the general assembly for permission to conduct a lottery. After granting authority, the directors or commissioners would organize the lottery, print the tickets, and conduct as many lotteries as necessary within the time permitted by the authority granted. On the given day, the tickets were drawn from boxes. Toward the end of the 1700s, rotating drums or lottery wheels began to replace the boxes. There were about one hundred lotteries held between 1783 and 1790 in the United States."

At that point, Mike Farrell paused and looked up from his brief. Because he was facing the nine justices, it was impossible for those in the gallery to see his expression; but he must have sensed the interest his introduction had elicited. He began to read from a reference.

His mother's hand fell away from her face.

"From Spofford, *Lotteries in American History*, Annual Report of the American Historical Association, 1892, pages 175 through 177: 'There can be no doubt about it—lotteries were an essential form of financing in the later colonial period . . . One hundred fifty-eight lottery licenses were granted between 1744 and 1774. Every colony and virtually every citizen had experience with lotteries and if there was any serious opposition to this form of money raising at this time, historians are unaware of it.' "

Mike Farrell returned to his brief.

"In the early 1800s, many of the new states also turned to lotteries to raise money. In 1823, Tennessee authorized a lottery to build a hospital in Nashville. Kentucky granted a franchise for a lottery in 1838 to raise money for a water supply system. Missouri passed a lottery to provide for firefighting equipment for the city of St. Louis. No fewer than fourteen states granted franchises to religious groups, including every major denomination, to benefit churches and schools. In the fifty years before the Civil War, numerous schools and colleges benefited from more than three hundred lotteries.

"In 1826, an aging Thomas Jefferson asked the Virginia legislature for authority to conduct a lottery to sell his assets to pay off his debts. The legislature granted the lottery, but Thomas Jefferson died before his financial problems were resolved."

His point made rather conclusively, that lotteries were an important, integral part of American history, Mike Farrell began to place his home state into the sequence.

"Mississippi was certainly a part of this early trend. As early as 1802, the Mississippi territorial legislature authorized a lottery for the establishment of Jefferson College. Consistent with the pattern in other states and territories, the Mississippi territorial legislature prohibited lotteries except those 'authorized by law.' Subsequent statutes continued to limit lotteries to those authorized by the legislature.

"Between 1810 and 1830, the Mississippi legislature granted more than twenty lotteries to various organizations to build schools, churches, roads, and to improve the navigation of rivers.

"From 1830 to 1865, our research did not locate any new lotteries," Mike Farrell added, almost as if he had just thought of it. "This apparent dry spell coincides with the reference in Professor Nelson Rose's book [*Gambling and the Law*] that the first era of widespread lotteries ended during the 1820s and 1830s with the spread of Jacksonian morality, aided by numerous well-published scandals."

Again he paused and looked at the justices, about to explain why lotteries became a "precise evil" that the framers of the state constitution sought to remedy, the well-prepared student presenting a thesis in a very tough class.

"The size of lotteries led to negative reaction. In 1826, there were one hundred sixty lottery establishments in New York City and over two hundred in Philadelphia in 1833 . . . The growth of lottery brokers eventually resulted. As the sums of money involved increased in size, professional ticket sellers—brokers—became full-time occupations. Brokers then started promoting their own lotteries after locating a sponsor and getting necessary legislative approval for a percentage of the proceeds. Lottery brokerage firms have been compared to Wall Street brokers of the present day.

"The end of the Civil War brought an immediate need for state revenues and a short-lived resurgence of lotteries in Mississippi . . . However, the post-Civil War lotteries were short-lived . . . During the 1880s, there was a scandal involving the Louisiana lottery that prompted a nationwide crackdown on lotteries. 'The blatant attempt by the promoters of the Louisiana lottery, a privately owned company, to buy the Louisiana state legislature resulted in the imposition of stiff federal laws and state constitutional restrictions.' Rose, *Gambling and the Law*, page 1."

That, Mike Farrell argued, was why Mississippi had constitutionally banned lotteries in 1869 and again in 1890. That was the "precise evil" the people had sought to remedy, not bingo.

"Bingo was not even introduced in this country until 1928," he went on, driving home his point. "By any stretch of the imagination, bingo could not have been perceived as the kind of evil that the constitutional writers were attempting to eliminate. If so, then 'lottery' would include all forms of gambling . . . Had our constitutional framers intended that result, they could have easily banned 'gambling' or 'games of chance.' They did not go that far; they simply banned what they knew in 1869 and 1890 to be lotteries."

Indeed, it did seem a compelling argument: how could the framers of the constitution have banned specifically what was not yet in existence?

Thereafter, Mike Farrell went after the authorities and the precedents the Attorney General had cited in his lawsuit, but the crux of his argument was clear: the court should peruse the history of lotteries in order to comprehend the framers' *intent*.

For a moment after Mike Farrell had concluded his presentation, Robert Malone again glanced over at Sue Hathorn. Then Jim Warren was recognized by the court and stood up to speak.

Jim Warren has thinning black hair that he brushes forward, a high forehead, protruding ears. Like very nearly every other man in the courtroom that day, he wore a dark suit and a tie. From the moment that he began to speak, it became clear in short order that Jim Warren did not give much weight to the history Mike Farrell had given and the framers' intent; rather, what concerned him was the "weight of authority," the *present* state of the law, how the law had been interpreted in the hundred years since the state constitution had been written.

"Contrary to the bingo operators' assertion," he began, "Section 98 of the state constitution prohibits any and all lotteries by whatever name . . . bingo *is* substantially similar in many respects to so-called traditional lotteries."

Jim Warren then went on to note that the similarity was particularly evident in light of the Supreme Court's own opinion in a case known as *Williams Furniture Company* v. *McComb Chamber of Commerce*. In that case, he recounted, some merchants had challenged a marketing-promotional scheme sponsored by other merchants. In that scheme, participating merchants gave numbered tickets to customers who purchased goods worth at least one dollar or who made a payment of at least one dollar on their store account. Customers whose ticket numbers matched the numbers on the prize tickets won cash prizes. The Supreme Court had not agreed with the plaintiff-merchants that the scheme constituted a form of lottery, and in their decision had set forth three essential elements of a lottery.

"Three essential elements are necessary to constitute a lottery," the Supreme Court's decision reads. "(1) The offering of a prize; (2) the awarding of a prize by chance; (3) the giving of consideration for the opportunity to win the prize; and all three of these elements must concur in order to constitute a lottery. The offering and the award of a prize by chance are not sufficient. There must be added, in order to make it a lottery, that the prize winner give a consideration for the opportunity to win the prize."

"Well, that sounds a whole lot like bingo to me," Jim Warren observed, but aware that the decision he had cited was itself a part of history, made as it was in 1927, sixty-three years before, he went on to explain that the "overwhelming majority of other states which have confronted this issue have held that bingo is a lottery prohibited under their respective state constitutions."

And he cited them.

"Indiana, Tennessee, South Carolina, Alabama, Kentucky, Kansas, Washington, Iowa, Wisconsin, Michigan, and Georgia."

And all *those* decisions were right up to date, made as recently as the year before.

"In sum," Jim Warren concluded, "the court must look at the plain meaning of Section 98—as opposed to construing the framers' intent—and hold that bingo is simply another form of lottery. That being the case, the legislature was without authority to exempt bingo, and as a consequence, the court should strike down as unconstitutional Section 97-33-51 of the Mississippi Code."

For a while, the justices asked questions of Mike Farrell and Jim Warren, asking them to clarify or to amplify certain aspects of their arguments. The questioning was polite, very nearly informal, and in that courtroom's cool, dispassionate light, it was easy to overlook just how much was at stake, literally tens of millions of dollars and all the lives so much money would undoubtedly affect. Not much later, the court ended its consideration of that case and moved on to another. The court would render its decision in its own time—the next day or the next year—and for the principals involved, there was nothing to do now but wait.

To any interested observer, lawyer or not, by whatever measure, after hearing the arguments presented pro and con, the case seemed too close to call.

37

*E*ven before the renovation was fully complete, even while, upstairs, the carpet man was stretching carpet in what once was a bedroom and now was an office, even while painters caulked and dabbed at the trim and a telephone installation person made final tests of the wires, Sue Hathorn was selecting the first of the furniture and getting it delivered, as she would say, "Fast, as in pronto!"

Already there had been calls about the center, about what it was there for and about when it would be ready for use. In response, Sue Hathorn had prepared a pamphlet entitled "The Children's Advocacy Center Program: Building a Community Response to Child Sexual Abuse," and when asked when the center would be ready, she invariably replied, "Why, we're ready right now." And because the need for the center was so great, almost immediately the house at 753 North President was put to use. In the evenings, a support group of mothers of victims of child sexual abuse met once a week; during the day, the first few children began to come in, brought there by parents who did not know what else to do, referred there by therapists and even a judge.

"Business is booming," Sue Hathorn would say grimly, "and we haven't even officially opened our doors yet—we're not too worried about running out of customers."

The goals of the center, as put forth in that first pamphlet, were "to provide a safe, warm, child-oriented facility to serve the needs of abused children and to prevent additional trauma to these children; to provide education, support, and other services to families of abused children, to assist them in regaining maximum functioning; to provide a neutral location for community agencies and professionals to meet for case coordination and case review; to provide training to enhance the skills of professionals who respond to child abuse cases; to coordinate and track investigative, treatment, and prosecutorial efforts; to hold more offenders accountable through improved case management." And depending upon the decision of the Supreme Court, all that *was* possible.

"For Sue," Robert Malone observed while helping to adjust the video monitor in the interview room, "getting this house is like getting a shiny new toy for Christmas. But without bingo, she ain't got the batteries to run it"—which was, all in all, with Christmas approaching, about as apt an analogy as was likely to be had.

In an effort to determine why she seemed on the verge of recanting, why in her interviews with the police and with the district attorney she had been uncooperative, the Youth Court judge ordered Tricia Alexander to undergo a few sessions with a therapist. The judge was aware that, when a child is not being adequately protected or reinforced, or when a child is being overquestioned, a not uncommon response is for them to become mute or to answer "I don't know" to questions they have previously answered. And once that denial is made, it is extremely difficult, both legally and psychologically, for either the court or the child later to sort out the truth. So the sessions with the therapist were ordered, and as it so happened, the therapist conducting these new interviews was one of the first to make use of Sue Hathorn's Children's Advocacy Center.

38

*F*rom the suburb on the outskirts of Jackson the foster-care lady again got on I-55, but this time she did not go as far as Pearl Street. She got off the interstate at Fortification Street and went on down to the right. Then she turned left onto North President Street and stopped in front of a house. The house didn't look any different from any other, really, except that out front there was a sign. There were a few steps up to the yard, then a short piece of sidewalk and then another few steps to the porch.

Inside, there was a desk near the door and a great big table in what probably had been the parlor. She was allowed to visit every single room in the house.

Upstairs, there were offices in what had been the bedrooms, but best of all was the room in the former dining room, downstairs, near the kitchen. A soft carpet covered the floor. There were stuffed animals and dolls and toys in the corners. There were games and a desk and a table her size. There were crayons and big stacks of paper and tall windows that let in the sunlight to all the soft and bright colors.

The therapist lady had told her that she could play with anything she wanted, up to and including the big puppy dog, Vachss, who had come out to greet her. She could sit on the floor or sit in a chair, it *didn't matter. She could play all she wanted to with the puppy as long as she didn't hurt him, and when he was tired there was all that other stuff to choose from. Totally awesome.*

The therapist lady sat on the floor and watched her. She asked questions sometimes, but she said that Tricia didn't have to answer if she didn't want to. She asked what she was doing when she played with the dolls, and almost every time she asked what she was drawing— she never asked directly "what had happened."

Down low on the walls there were drawings of sailboats and people swimming and on one of the shelves there was a play telephone, light yellow with a very long cord. When she picked it up to examine it more closely, the therapist lady asked her, "Who would you talk to if you could call up anybody you wanted? What would you tell them?"

"I'd call up my new daddy," Tricia replied. "I'd tell him to stop it."

After that she put the play telephone back on the shelf, and then she got to play some more, all by herself. She played with the dolls and the toys, and after a while she got around to Vachss again, too.

When the therapist lady came back and told her it was time for her to go—the foster-care lady was waiting—Tricia did not want to leave.

"When can I come back?" she asked very quickly. "Can I play with Vachss here again?"

"You can come back soon," the therapist lady promised. "And Vachss will be here then, too—he lives here."

After Tricia Alexander had left, looking back and waving the whole way into the car, Cathy Meeks said, "If some measure of this center is whether or not a child is willing to come back, I guess what we've got here is a great big success."

Sue Hathorn stepped up and hugged Cathy Meeks silently, without a sound, the two of them sharing a moment closed to all others, a sharing of feeling, a gathering of strength, a brief, very quiet celebration.

CHAPTER

39

*I*n the months that followed, there were various rumors about which way the Supreme Court was tending and about what Mike Moore was planning: the rumors scored the Supreme Court like a baseball game, 6–3, 5–4, 7–2, pro and con, and gave odds, as if it were a horse race; Mike Moore was rumored to be planning another raid on the Depot.

On November 8, Robert Malone was having lunch at a restaurant in Crystal Springs when the place was raided by the Attorney General's Office and the state police for running a casino-type gambling operation in a trailer out back. Robert Malone said hello to most of the Attorney General's investigators, since by then he knew them by name. That evening, while in the MCPCA office in Bingo Depot watching the news about the raid on TV, Robert observed that, while he did not wish his friends ill, the raid would make him a fair amount of money because, when gambling at the restaurant was started up again, the people running it would need new equipment to replace the roulette wheels and the craps tables that had been seized. When Sue Hathorn shot him a withering glance, Robert said, "Hey, Sue, it's *having* the equipment that's illegal, not *selling* it."

In December, Robert Malone and Sue Hathorn sponsored three different functions, each with its own very separate flavor. On December 13, they gave an open house at the center. That was a bittersweet affair because, while everyone who came was pleased with the house and was impressed by what had been accomplished, they were aware, too, that it would take quite a bit of money to run it. In the next week, there was a Christmas dinner for the employees of Bingo Depot and a Christmas lunch for the staff of the Mississippi Committee and the center.

The dinner for the employees was held at a local steak house, and the place was packed. Wives and husbands had been invited, and there were nearly a hundred people in attendance. The atmosphere there was genuinely celebratory, in the spirit of the holiday season. Gifts were exchanged and toasts were drunk until, toward the end of the evening, someone wondered aloud whether or not they would still have a job after Christmas.

The lunch for the staff was very quiet and restrained, a not out of the ordinary stop at the luncheon buffet at the nearby Ramada Inn—not out of the ordinary because the buffet was inexpensive and was a regular stop and because Sue Hathorn very nearly didn't make it. She had gotten hung up on the phone, then had an appointment, and arrived with hardly enough time to get down a quick salad and dessert. That done, she said Merry Christmas and was off again, talking into her cellular phone before she even got to her car.

On December 21, the Supreme Court handed down its decision.

40

*I*n 1990, Christmas Day fell on a Tuesday, so with Christmas Eve on a Monday most people were looking forward to a four-day weekend. They were making plans to visit family and friends and to finish up their last-minute shopping. That Friday, December 21, was a gray day, unseasonably warm, with the threat of rain in the moisture-heavy air. No one expected the Supreme Court to hand down its decision last thing on that Friday before a holiday weekend, and many people—including a substantial share of the local media—were caught by surprise. On another day, there might have been television crews and newspaper reporters and photographers to capture the moment, but as it was, Robert Malone was able to get a copy of the decision without anyone noticing and to go back to Bingo Depot to read it—he peeked at it, of course, but he wanted to be with Sue Hathorn when he read it all the way through. He called her from his truck and told her that he was coming.

To anyone passing by in that vast parking lot in front of Bingo Depot, going, say, to the drugstore or to class at the career college, it must have appeared that there had been some sort of escape en masse from a local mental health institution. There was Robert Malone, hopping around, dancing from one foot to the other and between whoops and yowls waving around a legal-size sheaf of papers. Sue Hathorn was right beside him, a bit more restrained but doing a good deal of hopping herself. Jeff Johns was there in his suit and tie, neither yowling nor hopping, as was Pat Brooks, the bingo manager, and Shannon Ware, Sue's new secretary. All of them were laughing and carrying on, or, as Sue Hathorn would put it, just beating the floor.

The Supreme Court's decision started out with an introduction and a factual background before it moved on to various other sections: an analysis, critical assessments, an acceptable premise, a summation, and a conclusion. Robert Malone had already read the court's conclusion, and from his mood it was pretty obvious what it was, but still he insisted on reading aloud the parts he liked as he flipped through the various sections on his way to the actual decision—and he had the only copy of the ruling. So with his impromptu audience gathered around him and picking up on his mood, each one of them with no small stake in the proceedings, Robert Malone read aloud, running his finger down the pages, stopping every now and then to let out a whoop or a laugh.

" '*The AG's Premise: A Critical Assessment,*' " he began, reading verbatim. " 'Close scrutiny of the opinions of the "weight of authority" reveals its employment of "loopified" or circular reasoning—which amounts to nothing more than unacceptable *ipse dixitism* or dogmatism.' "

Robert Malone paused long enough to ask of no one in particular, "Now what the fuck does *that* mean?"

"A Dixie what?" Sue Hathorn asked earnestly in reply.

" 'Restated,' " Robert Malone went on before anybody ran off to go get a dictionary, " 'courts in other jurisdictions have generally reasoned that bingo is a lottery simply *because that's what other courts have concluded.* In short, most courts which have addressed the issue have merely cross-referenced one another for authoritative support.' "

"You tell 'em, Judge Prather," Robert Malone added, refer-ring to Justice Lenore L. Prather, who had actually written the decision.

" 'This court cannot in clear conscience blindly concur in the conclusion that bingo is a lottery simply because other courts have so concluded. *Cf.* O. W. Holmes Jr., *The Path of the Law*, 10 HARV. L. REV. 456, 469 (1897). "It is revolting to have no better reason for a rule of law than that so it was laid down in the time of Henry IV. It is still more revolting if . . . the rule simply persists from blind imitation of the past.' "

"Revolting," Robert Malone agreed with the esteemed jus-tice, rolling his eyes.

" 'Reason can only help you get from point A to point B. But where did point A come from?' "

Robert Malone flipped the page, not at first glance really following that one.

" 'Accordingly, this court has perused dictionaries and other sources in search of the "popular" meaning of "lottery" and "bingo." Both games unquestionably inhere the elements of chance, consideration, and prize; however, this premise alone does not lead to the conclusion that both are one and the same.' "

"No kidding," Pat Brooks interjected.

" 'Indeed, the game of poker inheres the elements of chance, consideration, and prize. Does this mean that poker is a lottery? The AG contends (as does the "weight of authority") that *any* game which inheres the three elements is a lottery; therefore, the AG presumably would conclude that poker is a lottery. Indeed, under this broad definition, the stock market, life insur-ance, and other business enterprises involving the three elements could be deemed a lottery.' "

Reading ahead, Robert Malone gave a jump that turned into a hoot.

" 'Such logic seems no less absurd than that which equates a horse, dog, and cat with one another simply because each species has four legs, two eyes, and one tail.' "

"Get 'em, Lenore."

"Loopified," Jeff Johns agreed, as if he were hearing all right but was still back a section or two.

"'The absurdity stems from the unexplained recognition that the term "lottery" should be deemed the generic "umbrella" which encompasses any game (or business enterprise?) inhering the three elements. This court is unconvinced that the term "lottery" is a generic umbrella. The term "gambling" would seem to be the appropriate umbrella.'"

"Hell," Robert Malone interjected before he skipped on ahead, "I could have told them that."

"I think you did, Robert," Sue Hathorn noted.

For a moment, Robert Malone caught Sue Hathorn's glance and held it, both smiling broadly.

"'This court concludes that, pursuant to the "popular" meaning of the terms, *bingo* is not a *lottery*. This court's conclusion is reinforced by the structure and wording of Section 98 . . . any attempt to equate a bingo card with a lottery ticket would be superficial at best and unpersuasive at worst.'"

"Does that mean I get to keep my job?" Shannon Ware asked.

Robert Malone did not joke about the first sentence of the Supreme Court's conclusion but read it straight-faced. Then he let out a whoop that could be heard in the neighboring counties.

"'Based upon the foregoing, this court holds that bingo is not a lottery prohibited by the constitution, and the chancellor's decision is reversed.'"

Amid all the celebrating that followed—amid all the hugs and laughter and whoops and yowls and animated rereadings of the Supreme Court's decision, amid all the talk about what a Christmas present *this* was and how, at last, they were *legal*— at one point Sue Hathorn stood off to the side by herself and just watched the carrying-on among the people with whom, more than any other, she had shared this particular trial.

"God help me," she said, just barely audibly, a slight smile on her face, in her heart convinced that He had.

41

At the large conference table placed in the front corner of his corner office that has the spectacular view of the state capitol, Mike Moore leans back in his chair, and asks, "I mean, what did he win? What victory? What did Mike Farrell do for his client? I bet he paid. I bet you that Malone paid Farrell *lots* of money. And the majority of that money probably came from bingo business. What did he win for his client? . . . It's a question of people claiming victory, we won and we did great things for our client. What did they do? What did he win? Bingo is not a lottery in Mississippi. How does that help Robert Malone? He's indicted. He's charged with racketeering, still. He's paid large sums of money for a lawyer. He's lost all the money that was taken from him in the raid. He's associated with this situation for ever and ever and ever."

The Attorney General sits forward quickly, a challenging move from the state's chief legal officer.

"What did he win?"

It is, from the man who initiated the lawsuit and tried very hard to win it himself, a very curious question, one that Mike Farrell and Robert Malone and Sue Hathorn are all very glad to have the opportunity to answer.

42

As usual, Mike Farrell is very quiet and restrained, thoughtful, careful to be very thorough in his answer. Previously, to his credit he has made sure to point out that the Supreme Court did not accept his argument either. While he had maintained in his brief that it was requisite for the court to try to understand what had motivated those who had written the constitution, the Supreme Court had, in fact, ruled that they would ask "what the language means, not what the framers intended."

"Metro Charities decided not to start up again," Mike Farrell begins.

He is so soft-spoken that were it not for the preceding events and the pit bull-like way he conducted them, always moving forward, charging ahead, never backing down even half a step, he could easily be mistaken for timid, even shy.

"That was Robert's decision, simply because it, Metro Charities, had taken so much heat and had attracted so much publicity that it would be a lot easier to let the corporation not reactivate."

Mike Farrell allows himself a slight, sly smile.

"But Robert is still very much in the bingo business. He has his management and other contracts. He is very active. And he could not have done that under the terms of the temporary restraining order. He had a court order that said: do not play bingo. That court order was in effect from January 10 until about May 5, when it was lifted pending appeal. Had we lost the lawsuit in the Supreme Court, that injunction would have been made permanent and Robert could not have engaged in the bingo business in any way, directly or indirectly."

Mike Farrell shifts in his chair, smooths down his tie.

"In terms of the lawsuit, Mike Moore created this dark cloud over bingo and affected many other people—the Knights of Columbus, the American Legion, the VFW, the Shriners, and other organizations that play. During the lawsuit, some of them decided voluntarily not to play. They are all now able to resume operations. And that's simply because Mike Moore got beaten in the lawsuit. And Robert can lend his management and consultant services to any of those organizations that want to play. Metro Charities itself could play. We still think it qualified as a civic nonprofit organization."

Seated beside Mike Farrell, Robert Malone had been quiet about as long as he could stand.

"Let me explain why there's no Metro Charities," he begins, his voice as emotional as Mike Farrell's had been restrained. He stubs out his cigarette while exhaling smoke through his nose. "There's no Metro Charities because Mike Moore seized our bank accounts and he held them and filed his lawsuits. He created legal expenses to try to break me, even down to a comment that Jim Warren made, that I would run out of money way before they ran out of lawyers, because they had about fifty-two lawyers up there and they could out-money me 'til the end. They took all of Metro Charities money and assets and would not even let Metro Charities pay all its legitimate bills. We asked that we not get any money, just pay the bills that the checks were written on before they seized the money, legitimate expenses, electricity, rent, so forth. We went into court with a separate motion to ask that those expenses be paid; they fought with everything they had to keep those expenses from being paid

. . . So it was obvious that they zeroed in on Metro Charities to try to break 'em, which they did a pretty good job of. When they gave the okay to go back in the bingo business, Metro Charities didn't have anything. The equipment the state had. The money the state had. Metro Charities had nothing.''

Robert Malone twists his hand back and forth in a way that shifts the gold bracelet he wears on his wrist, allowing it to slide down toward this hand.

''I'm in the bingo supply business, too, don't forget,'' he goes on. ''Without bingo, there is no bingo supply. I have an interest from the supply point of view, and I'm a consultant . . . And I still have a place in my heart for all the charities in the state that make their money from bingo. And it just happened that I was the one that ended up leading the battle.''

When asked what she had won, Sue Hathorn's answer was much more succinct.

''I got my center,'' she said. ''Now I have the money to run it. We may not be able to help every child. God knows, we may not even be able to help most of them, but one child at a time, we *will* make a difference.''

CHAPTER

43

*I*t is January 10, 1991, a little over two weeks after the Supreme Court's decision. Robert Malone and Sue Hathorn are in Robert's truck making a bingo run, checking out their share of the local bingo business, when suddenly Robert remembers what day it is.

"Hey, Sue," he asks. "You know what today is?"

Not waiting for her to reply, using the telephone mounted on the dashboard, excitedly he calls Bingo Depot. When the phone is answered, he orders, "Put me through to Pat."

Without delay, the call is put through.

Robert switches over to the speaker phone so that Sue can hear, too.

Sue Hathorn is still trying to figure out what day it is. So much has happened, so much *is* happening, most days she can't recall what she had for breakfast.

"Pat," Robert says when Pat Brooks comes on the line, "ask 'em if they know what today is. Hold the phone up so that I can hear."

In that fancy truck with all the gauges and the soft blue light coming from them, rolling down I-55, it is strange to hear the sounds of Bingo Depot, the low murmuring of the players, the steady rhythm of the numbers being called. Then Pat Brooks's voice booms out on the PA.

"Does anybody know what today is?"

The crowd is not taken by surprise. Some nights Pat asks who is carrying a toothbrush or who has a wire coat hanger and gives a free game pack to whoever can produce one the fastest.

"It's the anniversary," a man calls out.

"The anniversary of what?" Pat asks.

"The anniversary of the raid. One year ago today. Right here."

"How about that?" Pat Brooks says, then into the phone, "Do you want me to give him a free game?"

"No," Robert Malone replies. "Give the *whole place* a free game."

"Now, Robert," Sue Hathorn begins, not yet accustomed to largess, still finding herself slowing down when she spots an aluminum can. But she is interrupted by the hoots and hollers and laughter that greet Pat Brooks's announcement of a free game.

"That one's for Mike Moore," Robert tells Sue, then to Pat Brooks: "Tell 'em that, Pat. That one is for Mike Moore. Maybe they'll remember it come election day."

"Maybe," Sue Hathorn agrees, not wanting to take away Robert's moment. "Maybe they will," she adds hopefully, though she doubts it. Heck, most people—even once they know it—they can't remember what's happening to so many children.

44

*E*lection day had come and gone in Mississippi by the time Dr. Cathy Meeks was called to testify before the Joint Committee on Performance Evaluation and Expenditure Review of the Mississippi state legislature. The Joint Committee was conducting a hearing relative to the Department of Human Services, though insofar as the state's children were concerned, the problem was already obvious: the Child Protection Division of the Department of Human Services had a budget of just over $4 million. In comparison, in Louisiana and Alabama, the states neighboring Mississippi on the west and the east, the budgets for similar services were $42.6 million and $40.7 million, respectively. Cathy Meeks read a prepared statement to the Joint Committee that she will later amend and combine with other speeches and use when she addresses the MCPCA's annual conference on child abuse in April 1992. In it, she tries to explain what the Children's Advocacy Center is all about, what she feels it has come to mean and to be in the sixteen months it has officially been open. In substance, this speech is not so much different from many other speeches she has given and will give. Even as the words change, the message remains the same.

When she is reading, Cathy Meeks's voice is clear and firm. When she is reading, as opposed to speaking extemporaneously, her eyes do not shut for that fraction of a second longer than a blink.

"As a psychologist working in Mississippi for the last eight years," she begins, "I have worked with hundreds of children who have been served by the Department of Human Services. In the last nine months alone, I have treated or evaluated more than seventy-five children who were in the custody of DHS. Most, if not all, of these children have been the victims of physical or sexual abuse. My work with abused children involves interviewing them to determine the facts of the abuse and to diagnose the extent of the trauma they have suffered. I treat children in therapy to help them recover from the traumas of abuse."

Dr. Meeks stands up very straight as she speaks. Her hands grasp the edge of the podium.

"Each of us who work with abused children sees a slightly different facet or aspect of the child's experience. The social worker sees the child where he or she lives, the context, the environment, the family. I do not know what it is like to go into a home and to find a child living in filth with no food and no clothes or to have to face an abusive mother or father and experience the fear for my own life, to see the agony of the child as he or she leaves the only home they have ever known. Nor do I know what it is like to be a police officer called to the scene of domestic violence or what it is like to be an attorney or a judge who spends hours working on a case to protect a child I know has been abused, only to see the case destroyed because of some legal loophole that has nothing to do with the facts of the case or the truth of the matter. I do know, though, what it is like to be a child's therapist. I regularly treat young children who have been brutally raped or beaten repeatedly—I recently worked with a young child who watched his baby sister raped, beaten, and murdered by his stepfather. My work is no more important, nor less important, than any of the others who work with this population of children. It is merely different in some ways."

At a table near the podium, Sue Hathorn, no longer the director of the Children's Advocacy Center, looks on. She is listening carefully, considering both Cathy Meeks's words and the spirit that prompts them.

"And what I want to speak about today comes from the singular perspective that comes from listening, being with, consoling, and treating traumatized children. I invite you to see a small part of this world, but be aware, though, that all of us, as adults, have powerful natural defenses that prevent us from entering that world: we have, every one of us, constructed a fantasy about our own childhoods—and about childhood in general—that allows us to believe that childhood is a wonderful, carefree, fun-filled time. We have, every one of us, put out of our minds the fear, the sense of powerlessness, the overwhelming experiences of shame and the insecurity that we all experienced at times as children. It is necessary for us to do this. Otherwise, we could not function in our daily adult lives. And be aware, too, that these defenses we have constructed that allow us to function can also blind us. Unconsidered, they allow a denial that is so great it is sometimes hard to believe."

Cathy Meeks pauses long enough to look over her audience at the same time that she turns a page.

"Let me give you an example of what I mean. Did you know that, after World War II, reporters interviewed the German citizens who lived right outside the gates of the concentration camps? These people lived and worked within sight of the smokestacks at Dachau and Bergen-Belsen. And when these citizens were asked about their awareness of the atrocities committed on their very doorsteps, they said, 'What atrocities? We had no idea.' 'No idea?' the reporters asked. 'Hundreds of thousands of people go in, no one comes out? The smell of burning flesh all day long?' But if you don't see, if you exclude from your awareness the painful insight, then you do not ask further questions and you are freed from the responsibility of taking action—which is much of the point here, much of the problem.

"When I first began to work with abused children, I had experiences that were like frozen moments, nightmarish epiphanies, when in the midst of a child's revelation of the details of a rape or a sodomization or some other brutal horror I would feel for a moment as though I had come face to face with the manifestation of pure evil. At first I thought the amount of child abuse I was seeing was an aberration. At some point, though, I realized it was just a representation of the amount that was actually occurring. And when I began to put this together in my mind and to talk with other people about what I was seeing, I began to feel like a lunatic. Ten years ago, most people, even professionals, did not realize how much abuse was occurring. The denial was so strong—and I've said this a lot—that I felt like the child in 'The Emperor's New Clothes.'

"At any rate, I think that somehow I have been shown these things that not everyone sees for a reason. And the reason is that I'm supposed to do something about it. I don't want this to sound grandiose—I believe that every human on this planet has a purpose, and I am just fortunate enough, I think, to have discovered part of what mine is. If there is something that keeps me plugging away when I get to points of despair, it is that. This is my place. I'm supposed to be here. And if that is true, then I'll be given what I need to do it, and I always have been, on a large scale and in moment-to-moment experiences. Little miracles occur all the time that give hope. When a child gets better because therapy was successful or when a plan comes together and a court case works, those are little miracles. In many ways, the Children's Advocacy Center is itself a miracle, though in fact it is nothing more than a house, a house where professionals from child protective services, law enforcement, prosecution, mental health, medicine, and education can work together. It is a house for mutual support, of survivors, of families, of the professionals who can so easily burn out. The Children's Advocacy Center is a miracle that has grown out of love, the single antidote to evil—that it is there at all is something of a miracle. But it is, in one respect, a necessarily limited sort of miracle because all that we can hope for is to offer some hope, some help, some sense of 'you are not alone' to a single traumatized child. That is not achieved through wining court cases, although that is important, or through therapy techniques, which must be practiced, but through valuing and caring about each individual child as the precious gift that he or she is. In that respect, we will never make a difference in the 'problem' of child abuse, but we will certainly have some effect on that one child. And the importance of protecting these children, one child at a time, cannot be emphasized enough. Not only must we, as compassionate human beings, care about these children, but also we must protect them if we care about ourselves and about the future of our society. Abused children, left unprotected and untreated, grow up to be dysfunctional human beings. They populate our mental hospitals and our prisons; they fill our welfare rolls. They grow up to victimize their own children. Many abused children of today will be the rapists, the muggers, the armed robbers of tomorrow. Your children and my children will support them and suffer because of them in the next generation.

"In closing, I would like to read a brief quote from a woman named Sally Casper, a child abuse counselor. In *The Meaning of Life* she wrote, 'Sometimes the most valuable thing you can offer is not an answer but your presence, your being there to share the feeling of loneliness, your being there while someone goes on breathing in and out . . .' I believe that that is what the Children's Advocacy Center is all about, about being there, giving our best for the children as they go on breathing in and out, our best as professionals and our best as compassionate human beings, and if we ever lose that sense of purpose, I pray that we'll close our doors."

To date, the Children's Advocacy Center in Jackson, Mississippi, has yet to close its doors.

This is hardly the end to the story.

CHAPTER

45

As Robert Malone had anticipated, after the Supreme Court rendered its decision, charges against him in Greenville were dropped. The agreement with District Attorney Frank Carlton disposed of all remaining charges against Robert Malone, both civil and criminal.

"As a result [of the Supreme Court's decision]," Frank Carlton is quoted as saying by the *Delta Times Democrat*, "no one knows what the hell the status of the law is."

Later that same month, March 1991, addressing precisely that problem, Mississippi's Senate approved a bill that limited bingo to clearly defined charitable organizations and placed limits on the profits promoters could legally take from the games. The vote in the senate was 49–2, and the bill, which had been approved unanimously by the House, went back to the House for a review of changes.

In November 1991, Governor Ray Mabus, the man who had originally proposed the lottery, was defeated in his bid for reelection. Kirk Fordice, a political unknown, garnered 51 percent of the vote to become Mississippi's first Republican governor since Reconstruction, since before the new state capitol was built. Among his appointments, Governor Fordice would make changes that would shock even Sue Hathorn, who was, by then, pretty much sure that she had seen it all. In his bid to win election to the state Supreme Court, W. O. "Chet" Dillard, the Chancery Court judge whose decision about bingo the Supreme Court had reversed, was also defeated. Mike Moore, however, did win reelection to another four-year term. He remains the Attorney General for the state of Mississippi.

Before the Children's Advocacy Center had officially opened, Andrew Vachss, an attorney in New York City in private practice specializing in matters of juvenile justice and child abuse, in conjunction with Covy-Tucker Hill Kennels in Cotati, California, had provided the center with a German shepherd puppy. In Mr. Vachss's honor, the puppy was named Vachss (pronounced "Vax"), and thereafter he became an integral part of the center. Vachss was obedience-trained and licensed as a therapy dog and began to work with the children, easing their fears, providing the kind of support and unequivocal affection that no human being can quite muster.

Early in 1992, a seven-year-old girl was brought to the center for treatment. She had been sexually molested and was about to have to testify against the perpetrator in a preliminary hearing. She asked whether Vachss could go with her into court. The prosecutor in the case agreed to ask the judge. Predictably, counsel for the defendant objected, but Judge James W. Smith ruled that Vachss could sit with the child when she testified, and on January 7, 1992, Vachss became the first dog in the history of the state of Mississippi to be allowed to accompany a child into court to testify. With Vachss lying at her feet in the witness box, the little girl spoke in a loud and clear voice while she testified. As a result of her testimony, the defendant was bound over for prosecution. The judge refused to reduce his bail, and he remained in jail.

For several weeks before Vachss's court debut, Sue Hathorn had been lobbying the governor-elect about his forthcoming appointment of a new director for the Department of Human Services. She had in mind a doctor then in charge of mental health for Harris County, Texas, but the governor-elect had heard of Sue Hathorn and he shocked even her: he wanted to know if she would herself take over the 4,000-employee department responsible for, among other things, child and adult protection, adoption and foster care, child support enforcement, food stamps, Aid to Families with Dependent Children, emergency food distribution, emergency community services, aging services, and youth services.

Sue Hathorn was rocked back on her heels. She had been openly critical of what she saw as bureaucratic sluggishness in the department, and she saw that in a way her bluff was being called.

Two days after Vachss's appearance in court, on the steps of the Children's Advocacy Center at 753 North President, after first introducing himself to the ninety-six-pound German shepherd watching the proceedings with interest, Kirk Fordice appointed Sue Hathorn interim director of Mississippi's Department of Human Services. On January 14, 1992, Sue Hathorn took charge of DHS and on January 15, 1992, she received a letter from Armis E. Hawkins, presiding justice of the Supreme Court of Mississippi.

"I am sure that Governor Fordice has, and will, make some excellent appointments," Justice Hawkins's letter reads in part, "but there is no way he could appoint a person more suitable for a post than his choice for head of the state Department of Human Services."

On that same day, at Sue Hathorn's request, Dr. Cathy Meeks took over as executive director of the Children's Advocacy Center.

One week later, the Mississippi House of Representatives

voted 93–25 to repeal the 102-year-old constitutional ban on lotteries. Previously, the Senate, which had defeated the proposal five different times in their 1990 session, had already approved the measure.

The people of the state of Mississippi would vote to decide whether or not a lottery would be instituted.

Tricia Alexander remains in the care of the state. She is now ten years old. By the time a foster-care plan is developed for her and the rights of her biological parents are legally terminated, by the time she testifies in Criminal Court if charges are forthcoming against her stepfather and in Chancery Court if her mother decides to leave him, she could well remain in the state's care for another three to five years. By the time she is eligible for adoption, and if luck is with her for a change and someone does decide to adopt her, by the time those proceedings are complete she could very easily be old enough to drive herself to her new home.

CHAPTER

46

Sue Hathorn is in her red car with red crushed-velvet seats—"funeral parlor seats," she calls them. Her driving is, to put it kindly, eccentric, a direct outward manifestation of her thoughts: she speeds up when her thoughts race ahead, slows down as she mulls something over, oblivious to traffic.

"Take a look at this," she says, digging around in a large canvas bag on the seat beside her until she finds the book she is looking for. "Look at the introduction."

The thin book she hands across is entitled *A Guide to Mississippi Youth Court* by D. Michael Featherstone. The passage she has referred to, and which is underlined in the book, reads: "In order to describe the modern Mississippi youth court it is necessary to place it in historical perspective. Our court, as are all youth courts, is the result of developments begun in the late 1300's in England when the *parens patriae* theory was utilized to give the king authority to protect those individuals who were incapable of caring for themselves. Among those so designated for such protection were idiots, lunatics, charities, and children."

"That about covers it," Sue Hathorn says, laughing. "Idiots, lunatics, charities, and children—you can decide for yourself who fits into what category."

Her car races ahead.

"Did you know that the very first case of child abuse prosecuted in this country was prosecuted under the cruelty to animals laws? The same man who took it on was the founder of the ASPCA. There weren't any laws to protect the children. They were chattel."

Sue Hathorn darts onto North President from Fortification.

"Here in Mississippi, up until a few years ago, in order for there to be child abuse under the law it had to be proved that there were broken bones or permanent disfigurement. So when a woman threw her baby off a bridge and it drowned, the case was thrown out of court. The judge said, well, there weren't any broken bones, and there wasn't any permanent disfigurement. Sorry."

Sue Hathorn pulls into the parking lot across the street from the Children's Advocacy Center.

"We've come a good ways, I suppose, but you see why we need a legal center for the children? You see why we have to hear their voices?"

She points at the house next door to the center, a similar house of about the same age and size.

"A woman owns that house. I've already looked into it. She doesn't know it, but she's going to sell it to us." Sue Hathorn pauses long enough to put the car out of gear. "She'll be glad to, once she knows that she's going to."

It is hard not to smile when you think, rearranging Sue Hathorn's own favorite expression: God help *her*.

About the Author

JAMES COLBERT was born and still lives in New Orleans. He is the author of four novels—*Profit and Sheen, No Special Hurry, Skinny Man,* and *All I Have Is Blue*—and numerous articles and reviews.